Love and its Vicissitudes

In *Love and its Vicissitudes* André Green and Gregorio Kohon draw on their extensive clinical experience to produce an insightful contribution to the psychoanalytic understanding of love.

In Part I, *To love or not to love – Eros and Eris*, André Green addresses some important questions: What is essential to love in life? What, in the psychoanalytic method, is related to it? Should we understand love by referring to its earliest and most primitive roots? Or should we take as our starting point the experience of the adult? He argues that while science has made no contribution to our understanding of love, art, literature and especially poetry are the best introduction to it. In Part II, *Love in a time of madness*, Gregorio Kohon provides a detailed clinical study of an individual suffering a psychotic breakdown. He describes how the exclusive as well as the intense lasting dependence to a primary carer create the conditions for a 'normal madness' to develop. This is not only at the source of later psychotic states and the perversions but also at the origin of all forms of love, as demonstrated in its re-appearance in the situation of transference.

Love and its Vicissitudes moves beyond conventional psychoanalytic discourse to provide a stimulating and revealing reflection on the place of love in psychoanalytic theory and practice.

André Green is a Training Analyst and Past President of the Paris Psychoanalytic Society, and an Honorary Member of the British Psychoanalytical Society. A prolific writer, his books include *The Fabric of Affect in the Psychoanalytic Discourse* and *Key Ideas for a Contemporary Psychoanalysis*.

Gregorio Kohon is a Training Analyst of the British Psychoanalytical Society. He has published and edited a number of books, including *The Dead Mother: The Work of André Green*.

Love and its Vicissitudes

André Green & Gregorio Kohon

LONDON AND NEW YORK

First published 2005
by Routledge
27 Church Road, Hove, East Sussex, BN3 2FA

Simultaneously published in the USA and Canada
by Routledge
270 Madison Avenue, New York, NY 10016

Transferred to Digital Printing 2009

Routledge is an imprint of the Taylor & Francis Group; an Informa business

© 2005 André Green & Gregorio Kohon

Typeset in Times by Regent Typesetting, London

Paperback cover design by Lisa Dynan

All rights reserved. No part of this book may be reprinted or reproduced or utilised in any form or by any electronic, mechanical, or other means, now known or hereafter invented, including photocopying and recording, or in any information storage or retrieval system, without permission in writing from the publishers.

British Library Cataloguing in Publication Data
A catalogue record for this book is available from the British Library

Library of Congress Cataloging-in-Publication Data
Green, André.
 Love and its vicissitudes
 André Green & Gregorio Kohon.– 1st ed.
   p. cm.
 Includes bibliographical references and index.
 ISBN 1-58391-744-6 (hardcover) -- ISBN 1-58391-745-4 (pbk.)
 1. Love. 2. Psychoanalysis. I. Kohon, Gregorio, 1943- II. Title.

BF175.5.L68G74 2005
152.4'1--dc22
                                                                         2005003044

ISBN 978-1-58391-745-9 (pbk)

Contents

About the authors   vi
Acknowledgements   vii
Foreword   ix
MARGOT WADDELL

PART I
To love or not to love: Eros and Eris   1
ANDRÉ GREEN

Addendum

PART II
Love in a time of madness   41
GREGORIO KOHON

From the analysis of a psychotic young man   43
The heroic achievement of sanity   62
'Between the fear of madness and the need to be mad'   84

Index   101

About the authors

André Green is a Training Analyst and Past President of the Paris Psychoanalytic Society, and an Honorary Member of the British Psychoanalytical Society. He was Visiting Professor for the Freud Memorial Chair, University College, London. At present, he is Honorary Professor at the Universidad de Buenos Aires, and Member of the Moscow Academy of Humanities Research. Since his first article written in 1955, he has published innumerable papers and a large number of books, some of which have been translated into English, among them *Private Madness*; *The Fabric of Affect in the Psychoanalytic Discourse*; *The Tragic Effect – The Oedipus Complex in Tragedy*; *The Work of the Negative*; *Chains of Eros – The Sexual in Psychoanalysis*; *Time in Psychoanalysis – Some Contradictory Aspects;* and *Key Ideas for a Contemporary Psychoanalysis.* He works in private practice in Paris.

Gregorio Kohon is a Training Analyst of the British Psychoanalytical Society. In 1988 he co-founded with Valli Shaio Kohon, the Brisbane Centre for Psychoanalytic Studies, which he directed until 1994. He has published *No Lost Certainties to be Recovered*; *The British School of Psychoanalysis – The Independent Tradition* (ed); and *The Dead Mother – The Work of André Green* (ed). He has also published three books of poetry in Spanish, and his novel *Papagayo Rojo, Pata de Palo* was finalist in the Fernando Lara Prize 2001, Planeta, Barcelona. He works in private practice in London.

Acknowledgements

The two papers included in this book are corrected and extended versions of the original ones presented at the English-Speaking Weekend Conference on *Love*, organised by the British Psychoanalytical Society in October 2000 at Regent's College, London. We would like to thank the British Society for having invited us to present our work, and to the people in the audience who contributed to the discussion.

'Love in a Time of Madness' was completed while participating in a Research Group on Borderline Phenomena (2000–2003), sponsored by the International Psychoanalytic Association. The members of the group were André Green (Chair), Jean-Claude Roland, Otto Kernberg, William I. Grossman, Fernando Urribarri, Jaime Lutenberg and Elizabeth Spillius-Bott. Gregorio Kohon is grateful to them for their comments on this paper during the discussions.

We would also thank Valli Shaio Kohon and Sebastián J. Kohon for their editorial help with the text.

André Green
Gregorio Kohon

Foreword

Love and its Vicissitudes is a scholarly and courageous revisiting of a subject that lies at the heart of some of the most exalted and debased dimensions of human experience. The book is an ambitious undertaking. As Green boldly and rightly says, the title is one 'that can summarise the history of psychoanalysis' (p. 9) – a claim that is borne out as these pages unfold. Yet this duo of monographs also moves beyond conventional psychoanalytic discourse and into new territories which defy tidy conceptualisation in any narrowly defined psychoanalytic terms. In each part, one finds oneself fully engaged not only with 'the wreath'd trellis of a working brain' (Keats, *Ode to Psyche*, l. 60), with two minds concentrating intently and brilliantly on their subject. One is also engaged (and very distinctively so) with two men for whom the subject stirs a sharp and wise reflectiveness – not only on the nature of psychoanalysis itself (its roots, its nature, its achievements and limitations) but also on the enthralling and terrifying nature of the phenomena of love itself. In so doing, they offer a re-exploration and repositioning of some of the fundamental principles of psychoanalytic theory and practice, reinfusing them with overlooked or scarce-remembered aspects of the more subversive and revolutionary dimensions, while also introducing some lesser known aspects of recent thinking. They grasp the nettle and seek expression for, among other things, the inseparability of passion from sexual desire, at-oneness, dissolution, loss, destruction, death, regeneration, madness – all compounded in that one simple word – Love. Each author engages with the mad-making contradictions of Eros and with the necessity of suffering it (that is, engaging with it, allowing and bearing it at all) without being cowed or overwhelmed by it. The two colossal concepts that bestride the book as a whole – each immanent in 'Love' – are 'passion' and 'madness'. The nature of passion is predominantly the preserve of the first part, and of madness the second. There are a great many common threads which constantly weave between the two.

For each author, to think about Eros is to explore the ability of psychoanalytic theory, heretofore, properly to engage with a vision of love, or to fail to do so. At one point, Green, having welcomed Lacan's crucial, and untranslatable, terms *hainamoration* (a statement of fusion, 'no love without hatred') and *jouissance*, regrets the failure to give us an articulate body of ideas about it. This volume provides the desideration.

As for Part 1, I shall be focusing on the significance of Green's choice of epigraphs and of the Addendum. This is not to mistake the part for the whole but rather to attempt to engage with one of his central tenets: that it is to literature that we must turn for enlightenment about the nature of Eros, in all its depth and complexity. In framing or situating his revisiting the place of love in psychoanalytic theory and practice, Green makes it absolutely clear that we are about to engage with the impossibility of disarticulating the chains of desire from the thrust towards life and passion on the one hand, and the concomitant pull towards its contradictory components on the other – ultimately those of hate, destruction and death. The links cannot be disarticulated because these polarities and contradictions are of their very essence. The roots of passion themselves engender, and are engendered by, the dark forces which are marshalled to oppose development and which forever urge the psyche towards defensive retreat. To learn from experience is premised on the capacity to *have* experience – and much of that sort of learning is akin, as Kohon argues, to a kind of madness.

Green frames his monograph with epigraphs drawn from Racine and Shakespeare and appends a reading of one of Shakespeare's most haunting and mysterious poems – *The Phoenix and the Turtle*. Each dramatist drew, again and again, on Greek mythology to encompass the elemental and enduring characteristics

Foreword xi

of the human condition. But Shakespeare's poetic oeuvre, here represented by *Venus and Adonis* and *The Phoenix and the Turtle* (or *Let the bird of loudest lay*, as it was known at the time) had a number of very distinctive and primary concerns. Many of them thread their way through the body of this book, explicitly in Green's case, implicitly in Kohon's. In establishing these points of reference, Green makes it clear that he is relating his own contemplation of love and its vicissitudes to the inspired modelling by the great poets of such themes as sexual desire; mixed or reversed gender; sacrifice and self-sacrifice; identity and loss of identity; enslavement, satiety, want and, ultimately, life and death. The poem may itself be 'about' some specific facet or facets of love, but it is also, *au fond*, so much more than this. For the rhythm, arrangement, sound and silence evoke what is not, and cannot otherwise be articulated.

The root of the very word 'poetry' is the Greek verb το ποίειν, to do or to make. It is a making in many senses, but perhaps primarily, as here, it is a making of the mind – the essential nature of development. Process, form and content are inseparable. The aesthetic dimension is necessary to enable intense feeling to be set before the eye of the mind sufficiently to be contemplated and for *a* meaning, always personally unique, to become available. This is Green's territory – one familiar to writers, artists and literary critics. Meg Harris Williams (1985: 36) is clear that 'The structure of an artistic form is such that it can capture meaning which lies outside its own terms of reference: thus in Book I, *The Dream*, Bion describes how a sculpture works on the observer: "The meaning is revealed by the pattern formed by the light thus trapped – not by the structure, the carved work itself" (1975).'

It has been suggested that Shakespeare's poems are not so much offshoots of the dramatic works, but rather those in which he 'undertook much of the foundational thought which underpins his dramatic work' (Burrow 2002: 5). Behind the narrative poems to which Green alludes, or on which he draws, lies a long tradition, much of it embedded in Ovid's *Metamorphoses,* of exploring the ways in which desire both transforms, but also warps, those who experience it. The mutuality (and mutability) of desire is both fundamentally disturbing and also ecstatic, transformational, even revelatory. The non-mutuality is deadly, destructive, malignantly all-consuming. Either and both are the stuff of madness; either and both are thoroughly dislocating forces, the innumerable versions of which are the stuff of great literature. To be able to be at one with the other, while yet to appreciate the otherness of the other, is a necessary, yet scarcely, perhaps only momentarily, attainable feat of human development (beautifully discussed by Kohon). It underlies the fate of Venus and Adonis and of Echo and Narcissus, sometimes explicitly, sometimes less so. The sense is that sexual fulfilment famishes the appetite it feeds:

> And yet not cloy thy lips with loathed satiety,
> But rather famish them amid their plenty
> (Shakespeare, *Venus and Adonis,* ll.19–20)

It is enshrined in some of the great stories of literature and mythology.

Such is the classic, narrative poetic genre for those vicissitudes of love which Green and Kohon are centrally exploring. It draws on a multiplicity of perspectives, and in so doing provides a model, loosely yet also precisely, for the enormous range of perspectives on which these authors also draw. Each, with characteristic panache and learning, challenges the constructive contributions as well as the limitations of one or other psychoanalytic tradition. There is a repeated and suggestive tendency towards a 'so far so good, yet . . . ' which continuously opens up further questions and possibilities rather than foreclosing them (*'La réponse est le malheur de la question'* as Maurice Blanchot put it) The multiple ways of reading and responding to the internal and external world are not patient of closure, nor of the confusion, between, for example, a hard, possessive, fantasising about, and a delicate, tender cherishing of, another; between the destructive egotism of some forms of grief, and the loneliness of unsharable experience. Here Eros is a force, incorporating the principles of love and strife. It is organically linked to its own destructive antagonist, each inseparably inhering, in myriad ways, in the human psyche.

Green's assured and succinct 'basic outline' and complementary critical analysis of different psychoanalytic positions, their strengths and shortcomings, yields to a focus on a difficulty that lies at the heart of psychoanalytic theorising. The fact is that the conceptual vocabulary of 'science' does not easily lend itself to the poetry of the inner world, especially to the core human experience of love. 'I think,' he writes, 'that art, mainly literature and especially poetry, undoubtedly gives a better introduction to the knowledge of love, which we grasp by intuition.' In *Poetic Diction*, Owen Barfield put this same matter particularly clearly. He said that 'meaning can never be conveyed from one person to another; words are not bottles; every individual must intuit meaning for himself, and the function of the poetic (and perhaps also of the interpretative) is to mediate such intuition by suitable suggestion' (1928: 138). As Green so rightly says, psychoanalytic models of the mind are rooted in 'the inspiration of the literary giants of the past'.

This perspective will briefly be my focus too. Little can be added to the subtlety of Green's reading of *The Phoenix and the Turtle*, nor to how convincingly he supports his view of what psychoanalysis can learn from poetry. He describes Shakespeare's consummate capacity to be inward with, and to find expression for, a level and type of mental activity which was, 300 years later, eventually theorised as 'primary process'. On this occasion, Green has not given explicit emphasis to what undoubtedly underlies his reading, that is to the nature of the aesthetic dimension itself; to the way in which it could be possible, precisely *because* this is poetry and not prose, to evoke the nature and force of something that would otherwise be inarticulable. The poem defies logical analysis. In many ways arcane, it remains, despite critical analysis, elusive, mysterious, almost mystical. The fact that it is possible to recognise in it an expression of the workings of the dynamic unconscious, of obvious interest to psychoanalysts, nevertheless tells us little about how it is that poetry alone could achieve this. One is certainly challenged. As Barbara Everett puts it: 'the reader halts, never quite sure what it is, to *read* this poem. We seem even while finding it exquisite, to lack some expertise, some password' (2001: 13). Ever elusive elements of meaning emerge momentarily from the form. Perhaps 'primary process', or the innermost and largely inaccessible workings of the human mind, might function as just such 'a password'.

It may be that, in part, the lingering elusiveness referred to resides in the many verbal innovations in the poem which, in turn, allow the lines constantly to slip not only between different registers (for example, the theological and the logical) but also between different voices, different identities, species, genders, possibilities, impossibilities. To generalise from a single line: 'Two distincts, division none' – here the form, the beat, the weight and sound of the words allow the poem to weld 'abstractions within the solid buttresses of "Two" and "none"' enabling physical, spiritual, even revelatory to interblend (see discussion by Colin Burrow 2002: 87).

Were Green to have drawn on the poem as a whole and not just on the 'Anthem', it would be clear that the arrangement itself brings into being suggestions of the content, not only in a line or a verse, but in its totality. For in the original collection, *Love's Martyr*, the final 'Threnos' was printed on a new page, with its own title, while yet being presented as implicitly a continuous, though also separate, part of the voice of Reason. I find this point of Burrow's convincing: '"*Let the bird of loudest lay*" is not only about the dissolution of separate identities into a single whole: it enacts it' (p. 88). The poem's metaphysical meditation on the sacrifices of identity in love and its apotheosis in death itself, the ecstatic and the deadly power of passion, speaks with an immediacy and with a kind of melancholy ferociousness to the heart of what Green has been saying and to what much psychoanalytic theorising has found it hard to keep a grip of. The sweep of Green's critique and his originality are rather breathtaking, and in its compact, scholarly and energetic style moves one's own thinking forward. The way in which his meaning is plucked from the lines of one of Shakespeare's most esoteric and profound works is a tour de force.

Part II, 'Love in a Time of Madness' is a tour de force of a different kind. It focuses on an extended account of the long (17 years) analysis of a psychotic young man, Tony. The reader is pitched into the living hell, both of the patient's madness and also of the extremes of psychoanalytic commitment and courage that are needed to sustain both analyst and patient through a treatment of this kind. In their different ways, both of them have to undergo, with and through the other, the fearful extremities of delusion, idealised transference-love and terror lest hatred and destruction supervene. Otherwise, the virulence of the illness '*of* hate and *for* love' (to draw on another resonant epigraph) might triumph and overthrow the necessary capacity to keep faith with the psychoanalytic method.

This beautifully crafted narrative traces a searingly detailed and moving story of suffering, of clinical and theoretical discipline, and of virtuosity. It is told by one who, to borrow from Keats, clearly dwells not in axioms but with the real experience felt upon the pulses, richly demonstrating the very capacities he is exploring – both for humility and for suffering.

While standing wholly independent, the clinical account functions as a kind of objective correlative for the allusive and elusive *Anthem* discussed by Green, thus drawing the two parts of the book together, not only formally in terms of subject, but more intimately in terms of the emotion underlying the content. There is a sense of shared meaning and profound accord between the two pieces. In Tony's delusional states, the impossibility of simultaneous at-one-ness and separateness and the terror induced by such a contradiction, become all too present a possibility, both inter- and intra-psychically.

(So they loved as love in twain,
Had the essence but in one
Two distincts, division none:
Number there in love was slain.)

Time and again, in this powerfully written clinical story, we become preoccupied, aghast even, at being pulled so near to the edge, as observers of, yet almost too as participants in, both murder and self-immolation. Just as, in the *Phoenix and the Turtle*, the quasi-metaphysical evocation of passion and destruction, of fusional unity and dislocation, is framed and contained by the poem's structure, rhythm and language, a similar evocation is framed and contained in the account of Tony's treatment (to the extent that such states can find any expression at all). This occurs both as a consequence of the reliability of the setting and of the analyst's capacity to stay with the psychoanalytic method. It is also the consequence of the patient's own capacity to write down verbal expressions of his fractured mental states and, eventually, to dream. Here too, then, symbol and metaphor enable the expression of meaning not otherwise articulable or accessible, thus marking 'the before unapprehended relations of things' (Barfield 1928: 67).

Central to each part is the absolute significance of infantile experience. Each author draws on the mother/baby relationship for the origins of the kind of passion and madness immanent in Love. At the same time, both of them contest the limitations of those theories that either stress the non-sexualised exclusiveness of such a couple, or draw on it as a primary model for the psychoanalytic encounter. They also contest the separation of the sexual mother and the feeding mother, the ongoing relationship between the two being rather a predicament, not only for the baby, but for the adult sexual being as well – and remaining so, in different manifestations, throughout life. Certainly the respective accounts, both of early experience and of analytic experience, persuasively move forward the debate on these matters.

For Tony, condemned early on by a mad mother to live with her (or in her) in a kind of delusional unity, his world wholly constructed for him by her, this meant that he had had no experience of the force which enables 'division' – that of the 'word of the father'. His life was a perversion of love, the destructive negation of Shakespeare's celebratory and elegiac poem. As Kohon says, 'He was a Royal prince, with no father.' He was left in a tormented confusion of gender and generation, of self and other, of sanity and madness. Stunningly, at one point, he receives a letter from his mother which begins, 'DANGER!! Jocasta calling!!' Traumatised because helplessly in the grip of such madness, Tony himself succumbed.

The absolute necessity in infancy of being enabled by another's mind to bear the extremes of love and hate as a 'normal' condition, a condition which generates the 'ordinary madness' of the infantile state, is described with exceptional vividness and sensitivity by Kohon. He shares Green's earlier view (1980) that this kind of 'madness' has a continuous presence in adult life. It infuses emotional experience in multifarious ways. It lies at the root of the capacity for passion and is linked to the vicissitudes of primordial Eros (p. 69) – 'madness' here, as described by Kohon, being distinct from psychosis and covering, as he points out, 'a multiplicity of phenomena, from insanity to rage, anger or violence'. 'To be mad,' he suggests, 'could cover being stupefied by fear or suffering; being carried away by enthusiasm or desire; infatuated; wildly excited; extravagant' (p. 70). Somehow, in his description of all this, Kohon manages to breathe life into the theories; he writes with an immense eloquence and clarity of thought and expression about the trauma of having no choice but to occupy a meaningless universe. There was no choice for Tony because no meaning had been reliably available of a sort that could distinguish love from hate, life from death, self from other, good from bad, sanity and madness. For, in turn, such a mind would have, enough of the time, to have been genuinely able to bear the distinction between, for example, love and possession – the origin of the state of "ontological contradiction" in which Kohon describes his patient, as the infant soul, to be living much of the time.

One further, significant characteristic of the complementarity of the two parts of the book is the common ease with which, enquiring rather than asserting, each author moves this way and that across the familiar, or traditional, boundaries of partisan psychoanalytical thinking. Clearly, their shared commitment to the search for a more proximate understanding of their central concept 'Love', of the psychic phenomena involved, and of the various ways of managing them with as much insight as possible, brings more closely together all those similarly involved themselves in such a quest. Partisan labels drop away and the truth of the experience of simply doing the thinking and doing the work speaks out. The richness of these reference points, as they are brought together to help understand such profoundly problematic areas of 'thought and work' imbues both parts with vivacity, warmth and a passion which is a rarity in psychoanalytic writing.

In the end, it becomes clear that what both Green and Kohon are grappling with is the nature of becoming more fully human, what constricts or liberates that process, the life conundrum that lies at the heart of much great literature, as of much philosophical discourse. It is the tragic predicament of being responsible yet not free, and the perennial conflict, defined by Winnicott (1963[1974]), and from which Kohon takes his *point de départ*, of being balanced between the fear of madness and the need to be mad. One cannot but feel that there is an appetite for life and learning on the part of each author (in their ways, poets both). By focusing their thoughts on Love, they speak to the analytic community while at the same time opening up, or shedding further light on, the nature of the human endeavour.

Margot Waddell
Psychoanalyst, Child Analyst and Consultant Child
and Adolescent Psychotherapist
Tavistock Clinic

References

Barfield, O. (1928) *Poetic Diction: A Study in Meaning*, London: Faber & Faber.
Bion, W. R. (1975) *A Memoir of the Future*, London: Karnac, 1991.
Burrow, C. (2002) *William Shakespeare: The Complete Sonnets and Poems*, Oxford: Oxford University Press.
Everett, B. (2001) 'Set Upon a Golden Bough to Sing: Shakespeare's Debt to Sidney in "The Phoenix and the Turtle"', *Times Literary Supplement* 5, 107:13–15.
Green, A. (1980) 'Passions and their Vicissitudes. On the relation between Madness and Psychosis', in *On Private Madness*, London: Hogarth, 1986.
Harris Williams, M. (1985) 'The Tiger and "O"; A Reading of Bion's *Memoir* and Autobiography', *Free Associations* 1: 35–36.
Keats, J. *John Keats, The Complete Poems,* Hammondsworth: Penguin Classics, 1988.
Winnicott, D. W. (1963 [1974]) 'Fear of Breakdown', in C. Winnicott, R. Shepherd and M. Davis (eds) *Psycho-Analytic Explorations*, London: Karnac.

Part I

To love or not to love: Eros and Eris

André Green

> Je le vis, je rougis, je pâlis à sa vue
> Un trouble s'éleva dans mon âme éperdue.
> > Jean Racine, *Phèdre*

> This sour informer, this bate-breeding spy,
> This canker that eats up love's tender spring,
> This carry-tale, dissentious jealousy,
> That sometime true news, sometime false doth bring
> Knocks at my heart, and whispers in mine ear,
> That if I love thee, I thy death should fear.
> > Shakespeare, *Venus and Adonis*

> Learning is but an adjunct to our self,
> And where we are our learning likewise is.
> > Shakespeare, *Love's Labour Lost*

Libido as an exponent – some questions

I would like to start by commenting on one sentence of Freud's *An Outline of Psychoanalysis:*

> The greater part of what we know about Eros – that is to say, about its exponent, the libido – has been gained from a study of the sexual function, which, indeed, on the prevailing view, even if not according to our theory, coincides with Eros.
> (1938: 151)

Let us briefly deconstruct this quote. *Libido* is not clearly defined in the text, except as it is related to instincts (quite a variety of them) and to the erotogenic zones; it is otherwise equated with sexual desire (1917a: 137). Eros has succeeded in overcoming the basic activity of its major opponent, the destructive instinct. Each of them combines in a fusion which can sometimes become defused. In the end, libido is '*the totally available energy of Eros*' (1938: 149, original italics) present at the beginning of life. *Exponent* is defined in the *Oxford Compact Dictionary* as: (1) 'a person who favours or promotes an ideal' – (2) 'a representative or practitioner of a professional activity' – (3) 'a person who explains or interprets something' – (4) '*Math*: a raised symbol indicating how many times it must be multiplied by itself'.

Note that Freud speaks here of a *sexual function* – and not of a theory of sexuality – because he restricts the label "theory" to the instincts as a concept related to inner forces, which encompasses different sorts of instincts and love relationships. The reference to Eros, which necessarily calls for an object, overcomes the earlier riddle: an instinct cannot be said to love an object (1915b). Therefore, by referring to Eros, Freud questions his earlier ideas about primary narcissism. The theoretical contents of Eros can be analysed as including: a function, its exponent, its components, its aims and binding, and its psychological counterpart. If discharge is still important for Freud, it has to be both related and opposed to binding.

The sentence of the *Outline* is an eloquent condensation of Freud's earlier views. Freud's description of falling in love and of what are usually labelled 'love relationships' is, in general, not particularly original. The originality lies in the theoretical statements which account for it. It is surprising that, in the *Studies in Hysteria*, four references to love out of five are written by Breuer (Breuer and Freud 1893–95). It is only after having written the *Three Essays* that Freud states, in a later study: 'In short, except for his reproductive power, a child has a fully developed capacity for love long before puberty' (1907c: 134). While he is quite aware of the exceedingly ambiguous nature of love (1925d: 38), he conceives of it as the result of the coming together of all the components of the sexual drive. It is interesting to quote the imaginary dialogue – a device frequently used by Freud – between a fictional ego and his respondent (1907c: 134): 'Nothing has entered into you from without that did not meet what was within.' (1907c: 142).

It is most important to note the description of the manifold manifestations of Eros at the end of *Group Psychology and Analysis of the Ego* (self love, love for parents and children, friendship, love for humanity), which Freud refuses to separate sharply (1921: 91–92). This helps us clarify our ideas about Freud's preconceptions. Eros is largely considered as an energy linked to instincts, fusing or defusing their expressions mainly through the erotogenic zones active since childhood, which, for most of them, in connection to objects, give birth to pleasure. Instincts are characterised by their conservative nature and are 'the ultimate cause of all activity' (1938: 148). They are known through different kinds of representations and affects, which contribute to give them expression and provide us with clues about their magnitude and strength.

The questions I will be dealing with in this paper, though not treated sequentially, are:

1   What, in the psychoanalytic method, is related to love and its relationships to other facts of psychic life?
2   In the teachings of psychoanalysis, what is essential to love in life?
3   What has the experience of life told us about love that we do not find in the work of psychoanalysts?
4   Are there other fields of knowledge, which can tell us as much – or more – than psychoanalysis, about this experience?

The immediate response that comes to mind is an answer to the fourth question. I think that art, mainly literature and especially poetry, undoubtedly gives a better introduction to the knowledge of love, which we grasp by intuition. These sources create a stronger and deeper impression than do psychoanalytic writings. The detour through imagination and poetic language of a very general human experience has proved to be more efficient than the ideas born from an experiment which has undeniably committed itself to the most constant and careful investigation of love relationships. To date, science has not contributed anything to our understanding of the core of the love experience, despite very limited findings on the somatic condition which precedes or accompanies the experience. At the other extreme, exceptional religious experiences and mythical narratives, mostly related to the writings of mystics, have shown to be closely linked to loving relationships (St John of the Cross, Saint Teresa, Jalal el Din Rumi, Orpheus). These sublimated expressions of love may be distorted by idealisation. The trouble is that when a psychoanalyst proceeds to de-idealisation love frequently ceases to be truly present in the communication. A certain dose of idealisation may be indispensable for those who want *to know* more about it. But is it really idealisation, or is it the need to use the evocative power of imagination to describe an experience which, told in ordinary terms, falls short of creating an empathic understanding?

It is as if the psychoanalytic view misses something which is lost in its description. The fact might seem surprising. Even if we were to consider that one of the contributions of psychoanalysis since Freud has been an extension of its traditional frontiers, bringing into its field features which were traditionally seen as pertaining to different areas, we could hardly find a better or more suitable topic than love as an experience, common to all human beings. Since the advent of psychoanalysis, the field of love has encompassed, as Freud said (1921), emotional experience which includes very different kinds of love, from infancy to old age, and from the individual to humanity at large. At this point, it might be useful to recall some important contributions from our discipline's history:

1   Freud's constant concern with the relationships between

sexuality and love. In fact, we can draw some conclusions which occasionally overstep this basic concern. With both sexuality and love, one always finds another pole with which they are coupled and opposed. We can say that sexuality has been the constant factor in more than a few multiple antagonistic entities. Sometimes the pair is internal to sexuality or love; sometimes it is opposed to them. At other times, the two perspectives may combine in an overlap. Examples include the opposition between sensuality and tenderness, narcissistic and object choice, love and hate, Eros and destruction, as well as different forms of love reunited in the concept of Eros.

2   Balint's refutation of primary narcissism, to which primary love is opposed.
3   Melanie Klein's emphasis on the predominance of destruction in the earliest periods of life.
4   Bion's introduction of knowledge as an organising reference on a par with love and hate.
5   Winnicott's refutation of the so-called death drive, which he proposed to substitute with 'ruthless love'.
6   Bowlby's theory of attachment.
7   Lacan's description of *hainamoration* (1972–73), offering once again a theoretical idea through a pun. The old French word *énamoration* (to be enamoured of), describing the state of being intensely in love is, in its first syllable, neatly homophonic with *haine* (hate). Thus the pun means hatred–*énamoration*. Lacan describes a feeling of hatred and love that cannot be dissociated, and for which I can find no better equivalent than 'lovatred' because, if we followed the French order of condensation, we would have an oxymoron, 'hatelove'. Seeing it in this order, as a single attached word, would reassert the distinct separation between the two feelings, which in Lacan's word are condensed.
8   We should also mention that no one has thought more thoroughly than Martin Bergmann (1987) about the determinants, evolution and contradictions of psychoanalysis with regard to love. Also, Kernberg (1995) attempted an evaluation of the couple in normality and pathology.

I will not enter into a detailed discussion of the differences and justifications of these main hypotheses. I nevertheless wished to remind the reader of them because, whatever our orientation may be, these ideas are at the back of our minds and are decisive in our choices and preferences.

On transference love

I shall now try to address my first question which refers to transference love, though I shall not linger on it as it has its specific literature which is constantly present in our minds. The topic could take up this entire chapter but I shall limit myself to a few points.

Transference was discovered in the *Studies in Hysteria* (Breuer and Freud 1893–95). Transference love has undergone successive interpretations by Freud (from being the burden of psychoanalysis to its motor propeller). It was completed with the discovery of countertransference, which, in some modern interpretations, is considered to precede transference (Neyraut 1974). Countertransference has been seen mostly as a combination of ambivalent feelings of hate and love. Sometimes, a surprising transformation occurs, and hate dominates the picture (Winnicott 1949c). Paula Heimann's famous 1950 paper changed our perspective, interpreting the patient's inability to communicate as a provoked reaction, thus making the analyst feel what the patient cannot express. The actual trend is to link, in a sort of couple that cannot be dissociated, transference and countertransference, as analysis is most frequently seen as a two-bodied relationship. This could be an opening for a wide discussion.

The question of negative transference has largely been debated from Freud onwards. In contemporary conceptions we see two antagonistic positions, extending from its dominance in certain transferences to its complete denial (when it is thought that the negative manifestations cannot be absent from the analytic relationship and have to be considered as substitutes of love). Negative transference is then only considered as an aspect of transference, not to be understood independently or as an entity in itself. It is interesting to observe that Freud's paper on transference love (1915a) deals with a special form of resistance in the transference

(Schafer 1993; Wallerstein 1993). Meltzer, trying to explore the outcome of psychoanalysis by examining, many years later, patients he had formerly analysed, observed an almost constant feature: a limited capacity for introjection and an always strong inclination towards transference which needed minimal circumstances to be reactivated at any moment. In some psychoanalytic schools, only transference interpretations can make analysis effective. This position is not shared everywhere. The distinction sometimes established in some conceptions is to differentiate between interpretations *in* the transference (any interpretation) and transference interpretations as such, that is, interpretations *of* the transference.

The widening scope of psychoanalysis since the late 1950s has led analysts, long after the works of Ferenczi and Rank (1924/1956), to recommend variations of technique: more concern and love (expressed more or less explicitly to the patient), deeper interpretations, symbolic interpretations, modifications of the setting, longer sessions, etc. There is no global evaluation of the changes brought about by the adoption of each of these new parameters. Today, having at our disposal a wide range of techniques, it is interesting to note that, whatever the other factors interfering with love may be, there is no view that denies its centrality in the cure, even if it is differently understood in the subgroups of contemporary psychoanalysts. Most of the time, the debates discuss the spontaneity of transference, or its appearance because of the implicit offer of the analyst who proposes the setting and places himself, willy-nilly, in a position that induces a love reaction from the patient. This may then become the strongest of resistances (MacAlpine 1950), and even be expressed through a violent hatred for a long time, before its hidden nature is recognised.

There is no doubt that contemporary clinical experience has confronted us with forms of fixated, sometimes unremovable 'love relationships', the destructive undertones of which we cannot be unaware. Is the reference to love still accurate or should we find a better word to describe the nature of the emotional links that are created in these analytic relationships (Bion 1962)? Nevertheless, this does not change the importance we attribute without hesitation to the loving experience. Should we consider a central state of love, around which all other aspects of loving relationships derive (or from where they are mixed with other fundamental feelings), or should we give up any idea of a single model accompanied by other forms revolving around it?

Post-Freudian questions on transference love

When discussing transference we cannot entirely dissociate what we think about it from this Freudian background. As far as love is concerned, it could seem paradoxical that, if transference is the lever of the analysis animated by love which always (except in the debatable case of narcissism) implies an object, how can we match this so-called solipsistic conception of Eros in Freud with the experience involving an object (transference) through which we can grasp its exponent?

Love and its Vicissitudes is a title that can summarise the history of psychoanalysis. Are the precursors of love part of it or do we have to consider them apart from love and the life cycle? Can infantile love be usefully taken as a model in understanding adult love? What are the links between various kinds of love (self-love, friendship, tenderness, sensuality)? What are the antagonisms to love (conflict between different kinds of love within its own field or conflicts between diverse categories opposing each other)? Do different categories of patients show modifications as regards loving manifestations? Should we understand love by referring to its earliest and most primitive roots, or should we accept to take our starting point from the experience of the adult? Most of the time, the choice of elaborating on the earliest and most primitive roots leads to leaning on reconstructions based on observation or theoretical assumptions. If we choose the adult model, we will have the opportunity to compare our findings based on transference with our observations of some pathological manifestations, our experience of life, our reading of literature and knowledge based on cultural experience. In this last instance, we are aware that we run the risk of falling into the traps of misunderstandings and misconceptions, mixing views belonging to different systems. The proposed advantage lies in the fact that the field of investigation is larger and that our identifications offer another source of reflection, even when these reactions refer to a more complex phenomenon, sometimes distant from ordinary experience. Without hesitation, if asked to choose, I will side with the latter view. If I prefer to take the viewpoint that starts from adult experience, it will prove necessary to proceed to retrospective constructions of its infantile roots, despite the risk of presenting ideas which go beyond observation.

However, observation is not always a guaranteed advantage but can instead be a limitation, as one has to select one among different approaches. Moreover, it leads us into traps where we become fascinated (I would even say nearly hypnotised) and inevitably misled, almost to the point of blindness, in the illusion of seeing what happens. I believe that psychoanalysis is the only discipline that enables us to understand more fully both life events which concern love (even if it is only, in general, retrospectively) and also how literature has enriched the experience.

We shall remain firmly on psychoanalytic ground, accepting at the outset that we must give up any historical survey or pretence of achieving more than a basic outline.

On being in love

Psychoanalysts, even with their experience of transference and their knowledge of their own and their patients' love life, cannot claim that their knowledge of love is greater than that born from culture (especially from writers and poets). Euripides, Shakespeare, Racine, Goethe, Stendhal, Baudelaire, Chekov, Strindberg, Proust, all continue to be the masters of psychoanalysts. It is not useless to try to describe the constellation of love the way they see it, even when they find it difficult to sort out the ideas and observable facts or hypotheses about its genesis, development, as well as its fall and decline. In any case, passion will be our model (Green 1986).

A psychoanalyst's first and probably strongest state of mind associated with the manifestations of love is the result of the lifting of repression. Something seems to have arisen from underground, as if it had broken the chains in which it was imprisoned, and is felt as an exalting liberation. It is difficult to say why, as in most instances the lover is already in love with some other person that will be abandoned for the new beloved. It may be that the love for the previous object was fading without the lover noticing it. But love at first sight may be an event akin to a revelation to a quiet mind. The main feature of love is a feeling of irresistible attraction, experienced in exaltation, and the desire to be as close as possible to the love object. When falling in love, the ordinary state of mind achieves a kind of mutation, as all writers describe. The most characteristic case is falling in love at first sight. But it also happens that love suddenly befalls the lover after some time – the beloved was known, but there were no signs that would have made it possible to foresee what was going to happen. It is felt as both inexplicable and, conversely, rationalised as totally determined. The lovers are predestined for each other, having waited a very long time to find their other half (Plato). A constant impression is not only that the encounter is perfectly harmonious but, in retrospect, must necessarily have happened. The love couple is said to have a fusional relationship: two bodies, one flesh. The couple is a new unity, unbreakable. Even when some ambivalent feelings remain from a previous pathological clinical picture, the new bond is experienced as stronger. Ambivalence may not be suppressed; it is first left aside. For what future? Impossible to predict. The feeling of a miracle overshadows the remnants of pathology. For how long? Impossible to say. From that point of view, symbolisation is a derivative of a love relationship (two broken halves which are joined together to form a *third*). In all this, appearance, vision, *revelation*, play an important role, peaking in the mystical relationship. The experience is felt like an opening to the other, and also to the world, if not the universe. This is not only fusion but immersion in the Great Whole, as well as a receptivity to stimuli which were, until then, silenced. Love is not only an opening of the senses but an exaltation of a sensitivity to the offerings of life. There is a feeling of being able to understand new aspects of life to which one was previously deaf and blind. In other words, love is a general opening of the being to the other, to one's own self, to the order of life and of all things that exist. One may distinguish between the qualities belonging to the state (being in love), the changes in the relation to the object, and the way the object is felt and perceived.

There is more to be said about the object. It is quite insufficient to emphasise its idealisation – and even to speak of an enlargement (as if the child's feelings to his parents were relived unconsciously). The main feature is irresistible attraction, painful separation, a colouring of any experience by the desire to make the love object fully and exclusively happy and protect it from any pain or harm. The object is felt as unique and irreplaceable. Therefore, it can call for self-sacrifice; the irony is that the love object is not credited with similar feelings, as jealousy – the green-eyed monster that mocks the meat it feeds on (*Othello*) – is frequently associated with being in love.

We may be struck by the extent to which oral metaphors come to mind in the form of hunger or insatiability ('She makes hungry where the more she satisfies', *Anthony and Cleopatra*). Was it not Freud, before anyone else, who said that the relationship to the breast was the prototype of all further loving relationships? (*The Ego and the Id*, 1923).

Of course, we notice the mysterious absence, the repression, of all negative feelings. It might be easier to grasp what is at play in the transformation of hate into love than love into hate, because the importance of the investment in the first phase (hate) can remain and persist under another form in its obverse (love). In any case, in both instances, we find the desire to be the exclusive benefactor, to possess, in order to endear, gratify or cherish, or harm and destroy. The transformation of love into hate is more mysterious. Eros has become Eris. In Greek mythology, Eris personifies dissent. It is the apple that was given by Paris to one of the competing goddesses, to indicate which was the most beautiful, that provoked the Trojan War. Aphrodite provoked enmity in the others. So we can see it, from this point of view, as a vicissitude of love born from jealousy. More broadly, dissent is what Freud is really writing about when referring to the unbinding action of the destructive drives as manifestations of the death instinct. It may be surmised that for structural reasons (narcissism), love is unbearable because it is consuming, unsure and precarious. It carries the possibility of betrayal. In the end, the love object cannot be trusted and there is great scepticism about whether the lover, more than the beloved, deserves to be loved.

It is debatable to think, like Freud, of a kind of depletion of the ego in favour of an overcathexis of the object as the only possible condition for love, as it has been noted that the loving ego can also appear enriched and elated, especially if the lover's feelings are shared (David 1971). The love experience is remarkable because of its exaltation, which very often leads those who witness the lover expressing his feelings to think that the manifestation of this passion is not reasonable. There is nothing one can do about this, beyond listening compassionately. Even transference love, in its excessive modes and understood by the analyst as a formidable resistance (including the negative feelings hidden from conscious expression), can lead to the same conclusion when interpretations only elicit feelings of helplessness in the loved party, and misunderstanding in the lover. Frequently, the lover seems to his friends, not to mention parents, to be making a fool of himself. This situation sometimes becomes a caricature when two analysands discuss how they see their psychoanalyst.

The attraction to the object (quite unlike what is called attachment) can be related to an overall state of excitement of all drive activities which Freud labelled as Eros in his later work. But mentioning all drive activities also includes aim inhibited drives, sublimation, etc. The part played by sexual drives which were not inhibited but only repressed or split off is a topic of discussion mainly for those who have preferred other bodies of theory (which do not even mention the distinction) to Freud's.

There is a need to be as close as possible to the love object, to have the impression that both minds, the lover's and the beloved's, are continually in permanent communication and, furthermore, understand each other even without the help of language, through shared emotions and intuitions, through telepathy. The very limited tolerance of separation and the common feeling that the two lovers are united in a way that cannot be dissociated in one body and soul are all accompanied by an irresistible inner certainty: that the lovers already knew each other long before they met. All these features plead in favour of the psychoanalytic conception that, in love, the lovers do not find an object in the object of their love but refind it after having lost it in the remote past. This reference to childhood, valued by all psychoanalysts, must also be completed with the opposite argument: that adult love has something new in it which gives to the experience of love a feeling that something unknown is coming to life. The increased communion of two bodies and souls may be understood in phenomenological and psychoanalytic terms as a modification of ego boundaries resulting in interpenetrations of beings: acute intolerance of separation or disagreement, intensifying and excitement of all the senses, loss of boundaries and lowering of censorship are almost constant. Even the body seems capable of being influenced and changed, explaining the role played by philtres in many legends.

Nevertheless, the new affects, travelling in both directions, are of a unique type; I propose to call this phenomenon *primary communication*, which sustains a mutually hypnotic relationship. This type of communication is largely dependent on an exchange of each partner's primary processes, which would explain the feelings of being two in one – itself a typical feature of primary processes (see Addendum). However, as close as the relationship may be, in the background we find an irresistible need to possess completely the object, which is felt as unique and irreplaceable, in the fullest possible way. This feeling, closely tied to the feeling of love, may be distorted, turned into jealousy or betrayal, and may engender the wish to be certain of being constantly present in the mind and person of the object (as if regressing to the state of part object). Most of the time, it is unconscious but it is not felt as such; rather it is only expressed as a mode of total abdication to the love object, expecting a symmetrical abdication on the part of the object. Euphoria is at the forefront of the love experience. When circumstances impose a separation, there is a strange modification of the experience of space and time, accompanied by longing and nostalgia, which emerge as the experience of time fluctuates in the alternation of presence and absence – the former too short and the latter too long. There is an immersion of feelings in the state of illusion, as long as love lasts. It is as if love had been invented to give human beings an idea of what happiness, if it could be permanent, would feel like! In *A Midsummer Night's Dream*, Hermia laments:

HERMIA O hell! to choose love by another's eyes. [her father's]
LYSANDER Or, if there were a sympathy in choice,
    War, death, or sickness did lay siege to it,

Making it momentary as a sound,
Swift as a shadow, short as any dream,
Brief as the lightning in the collied night,
That, in a spleen, unfolds both heaven and earth,
And ere a man hath power to say 'Behold!'
The jaws of darkness do devour it up:
So quick bright things come to confusion.
(*A Midsummer Night's Dream* I, 1. 140–150)

Sources, communication and changes of love

It is undeniable that the roots of love are already present in early infancy and develop later, undergoing many changes. Should we concentrate our understanding on better defining the earliest manifestations of love and observing its further transformations, or should we decide that, even if we are aware of the importance of the infantile experience, the main pattern is found in the love experience of the more mature individual in adulthood? This shift of emphasis would be in favour of relating the infantile experience to a retrospective view that would not limit itself to concentrating on the actual relation in infancy (as observed or reconstructed), but would try to deduce assumptions about what was already there in infancy, without being observable. We would be confronted with the more or less latent and incomplete expressions of love, that would only blossom in a more manifest, more complete, more total involvement, though no less mysterious and in fact more complex. It would be less describable within the limits of a direct communication from one person to another. An important fact about love is that it is not communicable, even when the love object shares the same feelings and experiences with the beloved. Even if we are aware that love changes over a long period of time, and that we could give a lot of thought to the modifications it undergoes, a mysterious event as important as love at first sight is its sudden extinction.

Needless to say, there have been many controversies, and not only about Freud's underlying biological preconceptions and his closed conceptions that neglect many other factors (the object). Freud was not forgetful, he was quite aware of the way he chose to express his ideas – intentionally and deliberately. If we do not know what love is, we can at least rely on our representations of it.

Ultimately, the experience of love teaches us that it is linked to illusion – and is eventually capable of turning into a delusion. It has all the possibilities of transforming the perception of the object, the affects linked to it, and the actions they entail, reaching sometimes irreversible consequences, from the happiest to the most destructive. Although it can be confronted, and even blended with it, love is not an outcome in the evolution of hatred (as stated in Kleinian literature); it is irreducibly specific, even if it can take different forms, more or less distant from the description of what is considered as its core. It can sometimes stand in close connection to its relationship to separation. Love is synonymous to reunion; therefore separation may seem unbearable.

Love is not a by-product of idealisation, though it can play a very important part in its formation. Winnicott understood the importance of illusion and disillusionment, which are different from idealisation. Love and hatred are, most of the time, mixed. This can be observed when the results of love are more ordinarily emotional. Hatred, as Lacan said, can be its most conspicuous character, as in *hainamoration* (lovatred). Love changes through time in the evolution of the individual and of society. It is a product of the transformation of childhood into adulthood, just as it is also transformed in old age (King 1980). These transformations are still very mysterious and neglected in literature. The main variations to the central core, as we have defined it, can depend on:

- The object (all the forms of Eros described by Freud).
- The central conflict between narcissism and object cathexis.
- The more or less predominant part played by the wish to control or master or get hold of the object as a possession (projective identification).
- Its relationship with sublimation, keeping in mind that sublimation involves a displacement of the aims of the sexual drives, an inhibition of sexual aims and the choice of culturally valued goals. The pull towards sublimation depends on the predominance of the attraction of the object. Irresistible attraction can block attempts to sublimate it.

- Love being opposed to mourning (David 1971). The happiness at the beginning of the love experience has its correspondence in the dullness and deadly state of mind of mourning.
- The opposition between love and hate on one hand, and indifference on the other. This must be understood in relation to narcissism and, in extreme situations, the de-objectalising function (Green 1999), just as negative narcissism must be differentiated from hatred.
- Love being, so to speak, the coronation of the object which has survived all the steps of infancy to reach the Oedipus complex.

Not that I ignore pre-Oedipal love (Bouvet 1967) but it is the full-blown Oedipal *structure* (as described by Freud in *The Ego and the Id*, 1923) with its double aspect (positive and negative), the combination of the difference between the sexes and the difference between the generations, bisexuality, the opposition between tenderness (the only erotic affect mentioned by Freud in his descriptions of the Oedipus complex) and hostility, the complementarity of desire and identification, which are the essential parameters of love. The extremes of love are reached in self-sacrifice for the sake of the object.

The Oedipus complex, transference and countertransference

There are claims to defend the idea that maternal love is the model for any loving relationship. To suppose that the Oedipus complex is the culmination of infantile sexuality, as Freud claimed, does not mean that his conception of the Oedipus complex is a matter of 'take it or leave it'. At the same time, I do not think that the neo-Kleinian *aggiornamento* is a convincing attempt to reconcile Klein and Freud. I will propose three possible concomitant versions of the Oedipus complex:

1   The complex seen from the child's point of view (with all the differences for girls and boys).
2   The complex as *Vaterkomplex*, corresponding to Freud's description of its correlate, the castration complex.

3　The complex as *Mutter Komplex* (Green 1992) with the observation that the mother is the only member of the triangle to have a bodily (carnal) relationship with the child and the father, without neglecting their differences. This is for me the matrix of love, with its danger-provoking developments.

One of the greatest mysteries of love is its ending. Why has love succumbed? Habit, selfishness, awakening and increased ambivalence all play a part. It is sad to observe that this is a very common fate. Nevertheless, as it endures over time, in some cases, tolerance to the other may become subject to variations; giving up the need to possess, replacing this with empathy, etc. can make for a happy relationship and not a sour one. The important parameter is how and whether the cathexis of the object is maintained (objectalising function).

To conclude, even if the conditions of a dual relationship are experienced to an unknown degree, I will include it in the general framework of *generalised triangulation relationship with a variable third* (Green 1995, 2000). This concept, born from psychoanalytic experience (including a couple with at least one other, which I call *the other of the object* which is not the subject), finds its source in C. S. Peirce's 'Thirdness' (1931).

It is impossible to understate love as a presence in the core of analytic experience. We are used to hearing, since Freud, that love transference is not essentially different from love in ordinary human relationships. Ida MacAlpine (1950) taught us that transference was not a spontaneous feeling emerging only from the patient, but that it happened because there was an implicit offer coming from the analyst. We might consider this reaction understandable, identifying ourselves with the poor wretches who throw themselves into the lion's jaws (in fact, we know they have little choice), or we might focus our criticism on the analytic technique which promotes what the analyst knows he is unable to satisfy. Transference love has qualities which we would interpret today as revealing an unconscious hostility. This characterises some transferences undermined not only by resistance, but also by a tonality of aggression of which the patient is unaware.

Generally speaking, I would like to keep in mind that transference and its manifestations linked to love are mostly unconscious. The patient is not only unaware of the part played by repetition but even, in his manifest feelings, is not conscious of the love undertones of his discourse, covering the field from seduction to passion. Even when he or she seems to detect the nature of his or her feelings, he or she does not clearly see what type of experience they are part of. This, in itself, is a justification for Freud's insistence that transference always has to be deduced – a good example for the debate on unconscious affect.

Sexuality and love have always been associated. This is not to say that they were always present together. Even when one member of the couple is apparently absent, his shadow is always in the background, sometimes leading to paradoxical situations: for instance, in ancient societies we have common prostitution commonly practised, but we also have *sacred* prostitution. On the other hand, mystical sacred love is now perceived as revealing a sexual component, the combination remaining a mystery – a greater mystery if one is not in agreement with psychoanalysis.

Freud's work was justified, in his own eyes, as in his time love was split from sexuality. He wanted to re-establish the connection but met many problems on his way that he tried to resolve, although sometimes by giving contradictory answers.

To speak of a constant conjunction is not to say that this conjunction is always accepted, recognised or tolerated. The combination can take many different forms, for example, the eroticism of the *Kama Sutra*, platonic love, sexual initiations for the training of people acting as intermediaries between the gods and the human in certain religions, courtly love, romanticism, etc. Each form and tradition has its code of what was recommended, allowed or forbidden. Moreover, up until recently, love was seen at one end only of the analytic relationship and was labelled as transference love. With experience, we have become aware of the importance of considering the analytic relationship as bipolar; that is, countertransference cannot be dissociated from transference, and it has become usual to speak of transference/countertransference relationships. We can discuss the precedence of countertransference or transference (Neyraut 1971). We can enlarge its scope and function (Heimann 1950; Racker 1968). We may shed light on the role of exchanges in the analytic relationship and question the neutrality of the analyst (Owen Renik). Nevertheless, a complete symmetry between transference and countertransference can never be defended, because the analyst has already been analysed. Even if he had a bad analysis, he has still been analysed (which does not mean that he can claim any authority on that basis). If there are many questions about the nature of countertransference, one has to keep in mind the distinction between countertransference broadly defined as the transference of the analyst onto the patient, and countertransference as that which goes against the development of transference neurosis. Love in the definition of the nature of countertransference does not imply a symmetrical relationship. Still, the classical method cannot avoid contradiction, when speaking of *benevolent* neutrality. Moreover, Winnicott (1949c) has shown the importance of the occurrence of hate in the countertransference.

The last Freud and the post-Freudians

Today's questions

Falling in love is a resurrection of a former state related to childhood, and the connection between the two needs to be understood. To find an object is to refind it (Freud 1925). While to fall in love with an object is to unearth a love which was first lived in childhood, we have also to consider its disguise through displacement, condensation, reversal, etc.

Psychoanalysts, especially after Freud, were divided on the topic of the relationship between sexuality and love. For Freud, two currents were to be distinguished, each following its own path: tenderness and sensuality, which would converge after puberty and adolescence. Other authors, starting with Balint (1965), defended the idea of a primary love, a concept which, being less precise about its relationship with sexuality, denied the existence of a state of primary objectless narcissism (Freud, Abraham). The great mystery still lies in the appearance, after puberty, of a conscious state where love is interpreted as falling in love, different in its manifestations from the other forms of love as remembered from childhood. More recently, Widlöcher (2000) has defended the separation between infantile sexuality and love.

As it is well known, sexuality can be seen as composed of more or less antagonistic aspects; it is the same for love (pre-genital-genital, part or total, narcissistic-object, self and other, primitive or sublimated, ruthless or concerned love, etc.). I will emphasise here two problems: the relationship between sexuality and destruction on one hand, and between love and hate on the other (taking for granted that, in the end, sexuality and love form a basic unity having to deal with destruction and hate).

Freud discovered very late, approximately in the last third of his work, that aggression (as in sadism) was different from destruction. He did not always feel the need to reformulate his previous conceptions, to bring them into harmony with his latest findings. So we have a mostly heterogeneous body of theory, marked by those later findings, without the necessary retrospective revisions to update his descriptions.

After Freud, the guidelines changed. Under the influence of clinical experience (of which he was not a fanatic), theoretical positions were modified. The contributors who are still worth considering on this topic include Ferenczi, Fairbairn (who did not like Freud's hedonism), Klein, Bion, Bowlby, Winnicott, Lacan and Bergmann. With Klein (and her follower Joan Riviere), sexuality was pushed back in favour of destructiveness. This also affected the understanding of sexuality itself (Rosenfeld, Meltzer). Bion postulated alpha elements (1962) as helping in the formation of the necessary material for the foundations of psychic life. Alpha elements were indispensable in the formation of dreams, myths and passion (and in some writings, also hallucinations and the narrative). One of his important contributions was the inclusion of knowledge at the same level as love and hate. Other currents tried to get rid of any reference to Freud's theory, instead of trying to improve it. An objectivist trend of growing importance now wishes to replace the traditional tools of psychoanalytic theory with others belonging to more 'serious' disciplines (psychology, more or less blended with cognitivism, biology, sociology). I consider this a great impoverishment of psychoanalytic thinking. The final word must lie with clinical experience, but this cannot speak for itself; it is open to different interpretations based on different axioms or hypotheses. Nevertheless, it forms the unavoidable basis for any further debates. Psychoanalysis is a fundamental science for knowing the human mind; it does not rely on other more basic disciplines of which it would be a by-product or application.

Biology has finally recognised that, as far as love is concerned, it cannot offer any answer (Vincent 1986). Scientists working in the field of affect have not, up to now, dared to offer a solution. The farthest point reached is the role of the genes which govern the favourable conditions for the transmission of the reproductive process (Wilson 1978, 1992). Anthropologists are becoming aware of how much the topic has been avoided, despite famous controversies. It seems there is now more willingness to open the debate. However, is it that we have the feeling that literature has got more to offer to the understanding of love? Is it that love rebels when confronted with analysis? I would say that love is a very appropriate topic to test psychoanalytic theories and show where and how they fail in their vision of love.

Though there are variations across time and place, we can still profitably read and think about writers and thinkers that other civilisations have produced. The variations also have the merit of showing us that we are able to recognise something that is still present in us, despite its remoteness. This leads us to the idea that changes follow different rhythms, according to the particular area where we observe them. Sexual mores are surely changing, but why, from a psychoanalyst's point of view, is the change slower here than in many other fields? And why do some changes seem superficial, and not affect the structure of the process?

In our present time there is a banalisation of sexuality which is, in fact, a denial about what is at stake; greater diffusion of forms of sexuality which were traditionally prohibited or at least silenced; a claim that any form of sexuality is acceptable, as prohibitions depended on questionable cultural choices, and an overall public excitement at the relief from ancient prejudice. But the point of view of a psychoanalyst is different because what he hears from his patients rings another bell. Also because, in fact, there is a general undervaluation of sexuality. It is our way of prohibiting a real questioning of the topic. With regard to love, the decline of religion and traditional values has fostered greater scepticism regarding the conventional conception of it. As far as psychoanalysis is concerned, there are very few books interested in trying to explore the difference between love during childhood and the love of the mature individual. The reference to the mother–baby relationship seems to split the mother from the woman who enjoys sexuality with an adult partner. *There* lies the real idealisation. Even in adult love, the choice of the reference model is rarely predicated on passion but more on stability, constancy and psychic equilibrium. In other words, once again tradition and puritanism have won the battle against Freud's conception, too hard to accept with its final postulation opposing love to destructiveness.

Klein and her followers – Winnicott

I will not address here the question of what repetition is and what is genuinely met as a new experience in the transference. There is something evidently new and different from its infantile roots in adult love, starting at adolescence. Here, we are at a crossroads between bodily factors (puberty), social relationships (discovering comradeship and fraternity), the modification of feelings towards parental images and, more than anything else, the qualitative transformation of emotions: attraction to an object which may become a love object, violence because of the activation of drives, attitudes of a more or less psychopathic nature (due to rebellion) and – as the Laufers (1984) have noticed – nostalgia for the lost pre-pubertal body. There is the intense need for and fear of close relationships.

The fusion between tenderness and sensuality after adolescence (Freud) is conspicuous, as is admiration for the love object (frequently reduced to idealisation). Admiration is immediately connected with the two previous currents. Needless to say, the mind's entire activity is converted to the service of love relationships, including sublimation – in itself a vicissitude, not only of sexuality, but also of love. This scenario, which is witnessed by older adults, with compassion or sometimes with contempt, can be re-experienced in more or less modified forms throughout life. All this includes the possibility of episodes of brief, mild madness, but can also lead, in other circumstances, to crime or suicide.

Freud's latest and greatest discovery concerned the inevitable fusion of love and hate and their possible defusion. Very early on (after the Rat Man analysis and the discovery of the anal phase), psychoanalysts expected as a matter of course that a certain dose of hate would be mixed with love. But the introduction of the death instinct and its corollary, primary masochism, changed the picture and raised, along with the question of primary narcissism, great resistance among psychoanalysts. Melanie Klein was almost the only one to accept Freud's vision. But she went beyond him. Not only did she accept the death instinct, but she turned the theory upside down, considering, for instance, that libidinal fantasies were by-products of the elaboration of destructive forces. Changes introduced by the neo-Kleinians, mainly to the Oedipus complex, resulted in a very questionable compromise when seen from a Freudian viewpoint. One exception to these theoretical changes deserves notice. Robert Stoller (1968), who had the misfortune of dying young, observed that, in the most 'normal' states of the expression of sexuality, a certain undertone of hostility was present. That observation has not been worked through enough.

Joan Riviere's work on love and hate is a classic of Kleinian literature (1991). Its weakness lies in the emphasis on the idea that love is tightly linked to reparation. Love cannot be confused with weeping over one's sins, having harmed the object. Mourning cannot be mixed up with passionate love. Love's melancholy is not attached to manic-depressive states, just as desire is not envy. Again, idealisation is not illusion. Freud's positivistic stand recommended us to give up our illusions. Winnicott was more realistic when he showed that illusion was indispensable, not only as a step to be overcome, but as a form of experience which survives, for instance, in cultural experience. Winnicott was not complacent in minimising the role of destruction, which also has to be revisited (Green 1999).

Winnicott defended two important ideas related to our discussion: he disagreed with the concept of a death instinct, whether Freud's or Klein's, preferring to qualify the aspects related to it as *ruthless love*, which trumps the capacity for concern. The second idea was about the instincts. He defended the concept of a progressive distinction from a primary state of fusion – the non-integrated state – where he thought it inappropriate to mention the drives. He did not deny their importance, contrary to many of his contemporaries, but defended the idea that some sort of primitive ego, not present at birth, needed to exist, to account for the experiences related to the drives. He did not undervalue them but simply believed that the infant must have found some sort of solution to these preliminary problems.

Freud in French psychoanalysis

Standing apart from these progressive and widespread ideas, French psychoanalysis on the whole, and more specifically Lacan, adopted a different position. When I say the French in general, I mean that, whatever their differences in their explanations or basic hypotheses, the idea that sexuality is of overall importance was generally accepted. Along with many other areas of disagreement, the American solution of regarding sexuality and aggression as factors of equal importance was not well received because of the difference the French thought existed between aggression and destruction.

With Lacan (1977), a new vision makes its appearance. Lacan focuses his theory on desire. Desire is at the centre of Freudian theory. He adds to it that desire is the desire of the other (the wish to be desired by the object as other), condensed with the idea of the other within oneself that decentres the subject and leads the dance – that is, the unconscious. Lacan joined this central idea with the notion of absence (of the breast), and created the categories of the real, the imaginary and the symbolic. He linked the unconscious with language (seen as a combination of absence and presence, the murder of the thing), and emphasised the difference between sexuality and love in both sexes. He also described '*hainamoration*', a form of love so intricately linked with hatred that it is not distinguishable from it (Lacan 1972–77).

In his *Seminars* (1972–73), Lacan reminded his students of his belief that the essence of love is narcissistic, and nurtures itself on its dissatisfied nature. Freud made a similar observation found in notes after his death, where he wrote:

> There is always something lacking for complete discharge and satisfaction – en attendant toujours quelque chose qui ne

> venait point – and this missing part, the reaction of orgasm, manifests itself in other spheres: in *absences*, outbreaks of laughing, weeping . . . and perhaps other ways. Once again infantile sexuality has fixed a model in this.
>
> (1938: 300)

This essential unsatisfactory limitation for reaching the climax of sexual excitation has its echo in love relationships:

> We are accustomed to say that every human being displays both male and female instinctual impulses, needs and attributes [. . .] if we assume it as a fact that each individual seeks to satisfy both male and female wishes in his sexual life, we are prepared for the possibility that those [two sets of] demands are not fulfilled by the same object, and that they interfere with each other unless they can be kept apart and each impulse guided into a particular channel that is suited to it.
>
> (Freud 1930: 106)

This led Freud to assert that every sexual relationship involved, in fact, four people.

In one of his famous formulations, Lacan says that there is no sexual relation (*rapport sexuel*) (1969–70, 1972–73). In sexuality, that is, the difference between the sexes cannot be determined by the concept of a prerequisite or predefined relationship. But he fails, having emphasised the importance of love, to give us an articulate body of ideas about it. In fact, it is impossible to understand Lacan without dealing with his concept of *jouissance*, which needs a long exposition. *Jouissance* does not exist in English. Language and our condition of being separate have to be linked with his concept of the other. It is similar to the concept of *hainamoration*. No love without hatred. That sums it up. Or to think of another epitaph: To love is to give something one does not have (possess) to someone who does not want it (the loved one). And Lacan puts on the lover's lips this definite statement: 'I ask you to refuse what I offer you because that's not it.'

It would be short-sighted to consider these examples as only reflecting a need to underline one's originality. In fact, these ideas reflect an entirely different view of analysis and an exclusion of our elaboration of what patients invite us to think about nowadays, where non-neurotic structures are so frequently met in our clinical experience.

Moreover, the shift of emphasis towards the early mother–baby relationship has had many consequences. The first is that it was assumed that it could serve as a key for understanding features which appeared long after it, forgetting that the end result cannot be a direct expression of the earliest relationship and bears the marks of the transformations undergone since the beginning, not to speak of those which are new. The final picture is composed of a mixture of different periods of development, a mixture of attraction for relationships and defences against them, a mixture of infantile sexuality and post-puberty sexuality, of changes in childhood and adolescent environmental conditions, etc. Another dramatic area of blindness is the disappearance of sexuality in mother–baby relationships, a point made by Freud and frequently undervalued, but which has been taken up again by some analysts, in different contexts, from Christian David and Joyce McDougall to Jean Laplanche, and shared by the majority of French analysts. In their reading of the current literature, the mother's sexual life is never mentioned, as if it had nothing to do with her relationship to her baby. To say it in one sentence, in ordinary life, mother and baby are in love with each other. I described one aspect of this complex relationship as 'maternal madness'. We thus have here a complex view: falling in love is a resurrection of a lost love object – not necessarily because it was murdered. Nevertheless, infantile love (though linked with infantile sexuality) undergoes a mutation in adult love which is, in its essence, basically the same as and fundamentally different from infantile love.

Brahma, his daughter and his sons

I shall end by relating an Indian myth. After having created his son born from his mind and then given birth to a daughter from his bosom, Brahma was so much in love with her that he could not detach his sight from her, so full of love and desire was he. 'What a beauty! What a beauty!' he endlessly repeated. This is why he is represented with four faces looking at the four cardinal points, to be able to continue watching her, wherever she stood. The gods, his sons, got so fed up with this situation, finding their father had lost his dignity, that two of them seized the young girl and took her away with them to the sky. Brahma then raised up another face on top of his head, following the girl until she became a tiny point on the horizon. Finally, having lost sight of her, Brahma became depressed, closed his ten eyes and developed hostile feelings towards his sons. One of them was still wandering around him: Kama, Desire, who stood facing his father with contempt. Brahma tried to conceal his fifth face under his hair. He was still repeating: 'What a beauty! What a beauty!' sighing in the company of his loved daughter Satarupa. He stood up and walked with her. He wanted to hide from his sons and make love to her. They did hide in a flower, sheltering their loving relationship for a hundred years. Shiva then appeared in disguise, and glimpsed Brahma's fifth face, which was not entirely masked by his hair. He got angry and lopped it off with his sharp nails. In fact, this fifth face threatened the balance of energy of the world. Thus did Shiva appearing in disguise behead Brahma. After that, Brahma became very angry. Then Shiva realised he had committed a great sin for which he was to pay a high price, having to become a beggar who would beg for his food in Brahma's cut-off skull (Matsy Purana 3, 30, 33, 36, 38, quoted by Roberto Calasso – 1996).

ADDENDUM

As we have said, the creation of poets goes far beyond the psychoanalytic interpretation of love; a very convincing example is to be found in the poetry of Shakespeare. Usually the Sonnets would come to mind. However, I wish to examine some verses of *The Phoenix and the Turtle,* Shakespeare's shortest poem – longer than a sonnet but shorter than his other poems.

Love hath reason, reason none

> One is always wrong
> truth begins with two
> (Nietzsche)

The Phoenix and the Turtle is one of the most mysterious poems Shakespeare ever wrote. Its sources are not fully identified. The poem was part of a compilation by Chester, called *Love's Martyr*, which included besides Shakespeare, Ben Jonson, Chapman and Marston. All of these poems tend to start from a theme.

In Shakespeare's poem, Dame Nature, at a council of the Roman gods, described the beauty of an Arabian Phoenix. She was worried that he would die without offspring. Jove answered that she would find a companion worthy of her on the Isle of Paphos. The meeting was postponed until the arrival of a Turtle (a turtle-dove), sorrowing for her companion, who had died. At that moment, Nature disappeared. The Phoenix and the Turtle then decided to die together in mutual sacrifice, for the sake of posterity. They gathered wood for their pyre. After some discussion about precedence, the Turtle entered the fire first. The Phoenix followed. A pelican that observed the scene was authorised to report their love.

Shakespeare accepted to be part of the group of poets led by Ben Jonson. Up to now, the comments about Shakespeare's contribution have been open to debate. For some, irony is the dominant characteristic, occasionally creating a feeling of mystification in the reader. For others, the poem is of priceless value, a consummate allegory and funeral elegy.

But what was Shakespeare's intention? Caroline Surgeon writes that 'from the large animal group, the outstanding point is [that] a great number [are] drawn from birds [. . .]. [In] Shakespeare [here], images from birds form by far the largest section drawn from any class of objects' (Surgeon 1975). Should we not bear in mind that when Shakespeare contributed to designing his paternal coat of arms, he borrowed from his mother's family and changed the figure? He replaced the original bird, quite similar to a turtle-dove, with a kind of hawk holding a spear (shake-spear). That does not account for the mystical atmosphere of the poem, which stems from the Phoenix and its very ancient myth. Though we do not know how aware Shakespeare was of it, we can deduce from his poem that he knew enough. Let us recall the essentials of the legend.

Mythological interpretation

The myth is supposed to be of Ethiopian origin. It is part of a Sun cult (in Ancient Egypt and Antiquity). The Phoenix is a bird the size of an eagle, of considerable proportions. His feathers are mostly red and gold, with a few blue ones. There is only one Phoenix living. He has a very long life (not less than 500 years). When he (or she) decides to die, he burns his nest – made of aromatic branches – in which he is consummated. In some versions the new Phoenix is born from the father's seed. The corpse is placed on the altar of the Temple of the Sun, where the priests of Heliopolis burn him (or her). The Phoenix stands exclusively on a palm tree (supposed to represent an image of perfection, associated with the solar cult). It is immortal and bisexual. It has survived in other religions (Islam) or in different countries (China).

One problem concerns its gender. In the poem, the Turtle is male and the Phoenix female. But in other contexts the Phoenix is represented as a super male figure. It does not matter: the Phoenix is immortal, bisexual and self-engendered. He is supposed to be free from the bonds of Venus. In order to be born he aspires to death (Delcourt 1992). He is addressed in this way:

> You are father and you are mother
> You are male and female
> You are voice and silence

The Phoenix combines unity and totality. The poem is composed of 13 quatrains and ends with a Threnos of 5 tiercets. The first part consists of six quatrains. It is an introduction about a Parliament of Birds gathering for a celebration. I will pay no attention to the poem's initial quatrains devoted to the ceremony, despite their symbolic interest, concentrating instead on the anthem (v. 21–52), which is the heart of the poem.

Remarks about some characters in the poem

Dame Nature

She is worried about the fact that the Phoenix might die without offspring. In natural terms, to copulate is a precondition for having children. She seems to ignore or forget that the Phoenix is a supernatural bird that is reborn after its death, re-engendered by itself. Jove indicates that in Paphos a possible mate could meet the Phoenix on a high hill, favouring the union. When the Turtle appears, Nature departs, as she has nothing to do with what follows. There is no mention of any of this in Shakespeare's poem. The Turtle is a male bird that is now a widower. He is mourning his companion and wishes to die.

The Phoenix and the Turtle

The main difference between the two is that for the Phoenix aspiration to death constitutes a condition for rebirth, as it is immortal. For the Turtle, death is the final end of life. But if they are burned together, this act of seemingly mutual suicide becomes an act of mystical union because of the Phoenix's divine nature. Thus, entering the fire first is a privilege. Following courtly manners, each invites the other to enter first, as if the fire were a bed of enjoyment (*jouissance*). The Turtle starts, the Phoenix follows. A pelican witnesses the scene in order to report it. This last sequence is not mentioned in the poem.

Literary interpretations

G. Wilson Knight, in a famous essay, *The Mutual Flame* (1955), brought together Shakespeare's *Sonnets* and *The Phoenix and the Turtle*, considering them to be a single group. The question of the sources, on which Wilson Knight tried to shed some light, is unimportant from our point of view. What is important is Shakespeare's treatment of passionate love. As Wilson Knight wrote: 'What we really want to decide is this: What meaning can the poem hold for *us*?' Many authors have treated the theme of the Phoenix: Petrarch,

Ronsard. Another source is Lactantius. The theme has frequently been interpreted by poets as an allegory of Christ. We find this in an anonymous poet of the eighth or ninth century. 'In Elizabethan poetry divine and human converge,' observed Wilson Knight. The poem conveys an atmosphere of mystical devotion: exalting love, including chastity linked to immortality. Thus we find a coexistence of contraries: the physical and the mystical are mixed. The equation Turtle – Dove = Poet is generally accepted. The Dove is a Venus bird, in contrast to the Phoenix, which is free from any bond with Venus. Wilson Knight believed the Dove to be male in the poem, but we expect it to be poetically female. We shall return to this.

There is a rich tradition related to the Phoenix. Hesiod, the Book of Job, Herodotus, Pliny, Petrarch all allude to it. In antiquity, the male connotation of the supernatural bird was dominant. In Spenser's *Hymns*, the Phoenix is the essence of Love–beauty, just as the Dove is the essence of Love–truth. Both are associated with chastity and exclude lust. That kind of love is platonic love and courtly love. In psychoanalytic terms we would speak of idealisation and sublimation. Many studies in contemporary criticism have developed the tradition. Each of the birds mentioned in the first stanzas describing the assembly has a symbolic meaning. They express chastity, royalty, immortality, non-sexual and bisexual unity.

Shakespeare's poem has been compared to the creation of other poets: Shelley, Donne, Lovelace, Michelangelo, Keats. Some of the authors who wrote poems which can be compared to Shakespeare's include Plato, Petrarch, Dante, Michelangelo, as well as Donne, Marvell, Shelley, Browning, Nietzsche. Quite often, the alchemists identified the Phoenix with the Philosopher's Stone.

F. T. Prince's 'Introduction' to the Arden Shakespeare edition of *The Poems* (1960) is also an important contribution. On many points, he disagreed with Wilson Knight. He underlined the 'suspicion of irony' throughout the poem *Love's Martyr,* as if the poet were participating in a private joke. In any case, *The Phoenix and the Turtle* shows Shakespeare's power of incarnation. What is supposed to convey mystical union is also very suggestive in Shakespeare of carnal love. Prince noticed that Shakespeare developed the theme as if it were a dramatic subject, projecting himself into it and describing what he saw. The poem shows 'unsurpassed musical imagination'. It is an example of 'pure poetry'. 'The beauty of the poem consists in a marriage between intense emotions and almost unintelligible fantasy. It is inexhaustible because it is inexplicable; and it is inexplicable because it is deliberately unreasonable, beyond and contrary to both nature and reason' (p. xliv). Prince denied Wilson Knight's idea of linking *The Phoenix and the Turtle* to the *Sonnets*. To find a convincing solution seems to be a real challenge.

The anthem: a psychoanalytic interpretation

Manifest content

The mythological explanation is related to the legend of the Phoenix with its supernatural characteristics. It is also concerned with the mythology associated with each kind of bird. Each bird is assigned a function in the forthcoming celebration. I will not consider all the implications of this symbolic presentation, and concentrate immediately on the anthem. After the two birds enter the fire:

> Love and constancy is dead
> Phoenix and the turtle fled
> In a mutual flame from hence.

The literary interpretation compares styles, and narratives underlining individual variations. This psychoanalytic interpretation will try to convey a comparison between the preceding approaches and the poem's meaning according to psychoanalytic theory. This is why only the anthem will be the object of this study.

The anthem extends from verse 25 to verse 52. Six quatrains are devoted to the love relationship and mutual sacrifice of Phoenix and Turtle. The fact that their death occurs in a consummation by fire is strongly related to the Phoenix. Here an ambiguity appears. In the poem, Dame Nature is worried about the possibility that the Phoenix might die without offspring. Yet according to the legend, the Phoenix must burn and live again out of its ashes in order to be reborn. So a contradictory meaning is attached to death for the two birds. For the Turtle death, in fact suicide, is a way of again meeting his wife, the lost female Turtle, which is mourned in the poem. For the Phoenix, it is a condition for resurrection. But their mutual flame has to be linked by passionate love. It is associated with chastity because it mixes an intense passionate relationship without any sensual participation and no consummation. It is the nature of this paradoxical relationship that invites the interest of a psychoanalyst. In Shakespeare's poem, the anthem is full of antitheses.

> So they loved as love in twain
> Had the essence but in one
> Two distinct division none
> Number there in love was slain

Number in love is *slain*. Number is murdered by love. It is double love (two parties take part in it), but so intensely that they form one single being. They are distinct parts and even so, are not divided.

> Hearts remote yet not asunder
> Distance and no space was seen
> Twixt this turtle and his queen
> But in them it were a wonder

Their hearts are separate and yet not distinct. This implies distance, but the space between the pair, between the Turtle and its queen, cannot be identified. It is clearly mentioned that the Phoenix here is female. Their relationship cannot be understood by others.

> So between them love did shine
> That the turtle saw his sight
> Flowing in the phoenix
> Either was the other's mine

There was so much love between them that the Turtle saw himself shining in the eyes of the Phoenix. Each was the treasure of the other. Sight here is reflected mutually, as under the influence of an internal flame. There is an abolition of the differences, not only between two partners but also between the sexes.

> Property was thus appalled
> That the self was not the same
> Single nature's double name
> Neither two nor one was called

Propriety was affronted, one self being also the other. One same nature named by two words. To name it as one, or as two, is equally inappropriate.

> Reason in itself confounded
> Saw division grow together
> To themselves yet either neither
> Simple were so well confounded

Reason is defeated, witnessing the whole born from multiplicity, each whole being his own self while also being the other.

> That it cried How true a twain
> Seemth make this concordance one!
> Love hath reason, reason none
> If what parts can so remain

Reason cries: 'What a perfect match!' For this couple that decided to unite 'Love hath reason' more than reason itself, if one remains after the separation of the couple.

The Threnos that reason writes in honour of the Phoenix and the Turtle is the manifest content concluding the anthem. We must note that they have no posterity because of their choice of chastity in marriage. The posterity is in the rebirth of the Phoenix. Truth and beauty have disappeared with their death. It is traditional to associate truth and faithfulness to the Turtle and beauty to the Phoenix (queen). Both qualities are rare, and are now in the ashes. The Phoenix will be born again and the Turtle will rest forever.

Latent content

Putting aside the fact that the poem is about the meeting of the Phoenix and the Turtle, the anthem can be read as a typical description of mystical passion and what is called today fusional love. It is in these circumstances that lovers feel they have one soul inhabiting two bodies. They know each other's thoughts even when they are separated or silent. They form a dual unity, are two in one, etc. Though each one is a 'single unity', when united as a couple they form an indivisible unit. The units are separated but in fact merge, come together. They can appear to be separate though they are not. It is a wondrous situation. Those who are not in love cannot understand it. Not only do the lovers see through each other's eyes but what they see in the other's eyes is their own image, adored and treasured. They belong to each other. The very principle of identity is overcome. They have two names but their nature is one. Each one is himself (or herself) and the other altogether. 'Love hath a reason' of a higher power, if what it divides remains whole all the same.

Wilson Knight thought that those lines needed little comment. In fact their polysemy is striking. We have seen that they are apt for describing passion, but we can also compare them to a meeting and mixing of love and death. Fusional relationships are a characteristic of the mother–infant relationship, whether it is interpreted as a narcissistic one or from the angle of an object relation. *A psychoanalyst can quote these lines to describe early relationships between mother and infant.* Up until now we have remained on the path of passion: the mutual flame between the Turtle and the Phoenix, the climax between lovers, the emotional mother–infant relation. We shall now mention another category that is indirectly connected with love.

In these verses, we find a poetical *description that reminds us of the characteristics of the primary processes* of the unconscious as set forth in the *Interpretation of Dreams*. The different aspects described in the poem are: *number* (oneness, twoness, distinction and division); *space* (distance or merging); *sight* (seeing or mirroring); *sameness* (difference, present or abolished; double meaning for a single thing); *fire* (mutual burning to ashes, implicitly the return to inert matter; or conception creating life).

Both are neither two, nor one. The negative is more appropriate than the positive: not *either*, *or*, but *neither*, *nor*. The meeting of a Turtle having lost its companion, mourning and waiting for a consolation, and a Phoenix having in mind its own posterity, supposes contradictory aims. In principle, the Dove wants to die in order to find once again its lost companion, whereas the Phoenix aspires to death for resurrection. For the Turtle, in the search for the lost object, the other is implied; only narcissism is at work for the Phoenix.

At this point we can no longer avoid the question of gender. The poem is explicit: the Phoenix is the queen of the Dove and the Turtle is the male. While in the legend the Phoenix is associated with many features pertaining to virility, in the poem – though bisexual – the Phoenix is female.

I suppose that Shakespeare was in fact thinking of the situation of a mourner, and then of a supernatural being wanting to give him back love by inflaming both souls. A new love is born from mourning on the one hand, and the exigencies of resurrection on the other. *The Phoenix is the poet* who never dies because his poetry is immortal and grants him a glorious posterity. His bisexuality is his possibility of identifying with both sexes; his femininity is linked with his creativity. He can die while sharing a new passion with the Turtle, to the point of making him forget his lost companion and consume himself, less in chastity than, to the contrary, in a carnal, transcendental relationship where he dies in the depths of ecstasy before being reborn through the achievement of the poet. Shakespeare's power is beyond reason because reason in him is ruled by love.

The mysterious thing is not Shakespeare writing about the Phoenix and the Turtle. For not only did he write the most inspired poem about supreme love, but killing two birds with one stone, gave the precursory *description of Freud's primary processes*. Then, we had to wait for nearly 300 years before they were spelled out.

References

Balint, M. (1965) *Primary Love and Psychoanalytic Technique*, London: Tavistock Publications.
Bergmann, M. (1987) *The Anatomy of Loving*, New York: Columbia University Press.
Bion, W. R. (1962) *Learning from Experience*, London: Heinemann.
Bouvet, M. (1967) 'I. La relation d'objet', in M. Bouvet *Œuvres Psychanalytiques*, Paris: Payot.

Breuer, J. and Freud, S. (1893–95) *Studies in Hysteria*, S.E. 2.
Calasso, R. (1996) *Ka*, Milano: A Delphi Edizioni.
David, C. (1971) *L'état amoureux*, Paris: Petite Bibliothèque Payot.
Delcourt, M. (1992) *Hermaphrodite: mythes et rites de la bisexualité dans l'Antiquité classique*, Paris: PUF.
Ferenczi, S. and Rank, O. (1924/1956) *The Development of Psychoanalysis*, New York: Dover.
Freud, S. (1907c) 'The sexual enlightenment of children', *S.E.* 9.
—— (1915a) 'Observations on transference love', in *Papers on Technique*, *S.E.* 12.
—— (1915b) 'Instincts and their vicissitudes', in *Papers on Metapsychology*, *S.E.* 14.
—— (1917a) 'A difficulty in the path of psycho-analysis', *S.E.* 17.
—— (1921) *Group Psychology and the Analysis of the Ego*, *S.E.* 18.
—— (1923) *The Ego and the Id*, *S.E.* 19.
—— (1925) Negation, *S.E.* 19.
—— (1925d) An Autobiographical Study, *S.E.* 20.
—— (1930) *Civilization and its Discontents*, *S.E.* 21.
—— (1938) *An Outline of Psychoanalysis*, *S.E.* 23.
Green, A. (1986) 'Passions and their vicissitudes', in A. Green *On Private Madness*, London: Hogarth Press.
—— (1992) 'The Oedipus complex as Mutter Komplex', in B. Juillert (ed.) *Shooting the Sun: Ritual and Meaning in West Sepik*, Washington: Smithsonian Institution Press, pp. 144–172.
—— (1995) *Propédeutique: la métapsychologie revisitée*, Seyssel: Editions Champ Vallon.
—— (1999) *The Work of the Negative*, trans. A. Weller, London: Free Association Books.
—— (2000) *Chains of Eros*, trans. A. Weller, London: Rebus Press.
—— (2001) *André Green at the Squiggle Foundation*, J. Abram, (ed.), London: Karnac.
—— (2002) 'La mort dans la vie', in A. Green *La pensée clinique*, Paris: Odile Jacob.
Heimann, P. (1950) 'On counter-transference', *International Journal of Psycho-Analysis* 31: 81–84.
Kernberg, O. (1995) *Love Relations – Normality and Pathology*, London: Yale University Press.
King, P. (1980) 'The life cycle as indicated by the nature of transference in the psychoanalysis of the middle-aged and elderly', *International Journal of Psycho-Analysis* 61: 153–160.
Klein, M. (1957) *Envy and Gratitude*, London: Tavistock Publications.
Klein, M. and Riviere, J. (1967) *Love, Hate and Reparation*, London: Hogarth Press.
Knight, G. Wilson (1955) *The Mutual Flame: On Shakespeare's Sonnets and The Phoenix and the Turtle*, London: Methuen.
Lacan, J. (1969–70) *Le Séminaire. Livre XVII. L'envers de la psychanalyse, 1969–70*, J.-A. Miller (ed.), Paris: Seuil, 1991.

—— (1972–73) *Le Séminaire. Livre XX. Encore, 1962–63*, J.-A. Miller (ed.), Paris: Seuil.
—— (1977) *Écrits. A Selection*, trans. by A. Sheridan, London: Tavistock Publications.
Laufer, M. and Laufer, E. (1984) *Adolescence and Developmental Breakdown: A Psychoanalytic View*, New York: Yale University Press.
MacAlpine, I. (1950) 'The development of transference', *Psychoanalytic Quarterly* 19: 509–539.
Neyraut, M. (1974) *Le transfert*, Paris: Presses Universitaires de France.
Peirce, S. C. (1931) 'Thirdness. The reality of thirdness', in *Collected Papers*. Book II. 1.343.345.347. Correspondence to Lady Welby. 8.327.341. Cambridge, MA: Harvard University Press.
Prince, F. T. (ed.) (1960) 'Introduction', in W. Shakespeare, *The Poems*, The Arden Shakepeare, London: Routledge.
Racker, H. (1968) *Transference and Counter-transference*, London: Hogarth Press.
Riviere, J. (1991) *The Inner World and Joan Riviere – Collected Papers: 1920–1958*, A. Hughes (ed.), London: Karnac.
Schafer, R. (1993) 'Five readings of Freud's "Observations on transference-love"', in *On Freud's 'Observations on Transference-Love'*, New Haven, CT: Yale University Press.
Stoller, R. (1968) *Sex and Gender*, New York: Science House.
Surgeon, C. (1975) *Shakespeare's Imagery*, Cambridge: Cambridge University Press.
Vincent, J. D. (1986) *Biologie des passions*, Paris: Odile Jacob.
Wallerstein, R. (1993) 'On transference love. Revisiting Freud', in *On Freud's 'Observations on Transference-Love'*, New Haven, CT: Yale University Press.
Widlöcher, D. (2000) 'Amour primaire et sexualité infantile', in D. Widlöcher *Sexualité infantile et attachement*, Paris: Presses Universitaires de France.
Wilson, E. (1978) *On Human Nature*, Cambridge, MA: Harvard University Press.
—— (1992) *The Diversity of Life*, Cambridge, MA: Harvard University Press.
Winnicott, D. W. (1949c) 'Hate in the countertransference', in D. W. Winnicott *Collected Papers: Through Paediatrics to Psychoanalysis*, London: Tavistock Publications, 1958.
—— (1971) *Playing and Reality*, London: Tavistock Publications.

Part II
Love in a time of madness

Gregorio Kohon

In memory of Liliana Rosa Kohon
30/10/1953–10/2/1971

> There is only one illness: we are all ill *of* hate and *for* love.
> (Enrique Pichon-Rivière, 1965)

FROM THE ANALYSIS OF A PSYCHOTIC YOUNG MAN

Although Tony could not trust his memory, he had always known that without memories he was nothing. He was aware that his past had been invented by his mother through a series of half-lies, illusions and self-deceptions that she presented to herself and to the world as truths. He no longer fought with his mother about this; he knew that to argue with her was a fruitless, painful exercise. His mother was not necessarily aware of her capacity for conjuring up people and events from the past in a way that did not even remotely reflect their reality. Tony knew she was mad, but he was unable to put this into words until some time later in his analysis.

The earliest memory Tony had was of a beer garden, in a country pub somewhere. He was playing on the swings with his sister while their mother and father drank, smoked, laughed and talked to other people. He could remember sensations: the suffocating smell of tobacco on his mother's winter coat, his father's rather loud voice calling to a friend across the tables, his sister's graceful and dignified movements on the swing, his own fear of swings. He could remember an afternoon spent on the stony beaches of Brighton: he saw himself eating a big, long piece of the pink rock that was sold at sweet shops by the esplanade. He was sitting by the sea, feeling hot, unhappy, crying about something he could not account for, becoming afraid.

In fact, fear was what he remembered the most: fear of his father, fear of school, fear of the teachers, fear of the water, fear of the swings, fear of cars. These fears paralysed him. He could not swim, he hated travelling, the mere thought of an aeroplane made him throw up. He felt defeated by his lack of courage. When the children at school called him names, he could imagine himself actually being transformed into a chicken, a rabbit, a rat. He would wake up at night sweating, shivering, seeing himself as a small animal floating on heavy seas, agitated and confused. He felt isolated. And yet it was these memories that gave him a sense of reassurance: after all, he was like anybody else, he had a family and a past. Life had some meaning.

The first time I saw Tony, it was in the context of a family interview, with his mother and elder sister. He had been referred to a colleague of mine who had invited me to participate as co-therapist. Tony was 21 years old; he had long hair, dirty clothes and a smell that made one sick. It permeated everything. After he left the room, a truly offensive, noxious stench lingered in the air.

After a violent public outburst in a crowded street, he had been picked up by the police – they had had to struggle to push him into one of their vans. Tony was diagnosed by the hospital psychiatrist as paranoid schizophrenic. He spent only three days in hospital, detained under the Mental Health Act; electroshock treatment had been strongly recommended. Nevertheless, his mother took him home after he begged her to support him in refusing treatment. She agreed. 'I want to save my boy,' she said to us. She offered to pay for one perhaps two years of psychotherapy.

Tony had been 'doing drugs' on a daily basis. I would later discover that at different times he had tried hashish and marihuana, mescaline, hallucinogenic mushrooms and LSD. Given the culture of the time (early 1970s), this was not completely unexpected, or unusual. He had used these drugs occasionally, for recreational and experimental purposes only; he was not addicted. Tony's breakdown had taken place after a bad trip with LSD. He started feeling as if he were outside his body; he thought people were after him. He developed strange body sensations: a spot on his head, for example, grew into a big penis that was out of control. He felt that the pavement was pulsating, the trees breathing. He looked at himself in the mirror and turned into Paul McCartney. He screamed at a Leonard Cohen record cover, claiming that the singer had stolen his face. He shouted in the street that he wanted his soul back inside his body. He sat for long hours in the house where he was squatting with friends, thinking that everyone around him was dead. He had terrifying nightmares, from which he found it difficult to awaken.

In the family interview, the mother did most of the talking, describing the family background and present circumstances. She dominated the scene and spoke on everybody's behalf. She was anxious, at times fairly manic; there was a histrionic side to her that made one feel part of the audience in a show. Tony's sister did not participate. Clearly, she did not want to be there; she had her own life and had her own problems to cope with. Tony said nothing and sat stiffly on his chair, looking lost. If asked anything, he responded mainly in mumbles and whispers. He kept his hands crossed over his stomach, as if holding himself in. From time to time, he would laugh with no apparent reason. At the end of the family consultation, it was suggested that Tony come to see me in therapy. He glanced at me with a mixture of despair and defiance. It was the beginning of a therapeutic relationship that was to last 17 years.

Tony had grown up in a more or less 'typical' family in a Manchester suburb. Father, a businessman, had died from a heart attack when Tony was in his teens, shortly after the family moved to London. Mother had been a teacher and was now retired. His only sister, 25 years old, left home at a young age to marry, but this did not last. While still living at home, she had spent a great deal of time complaining about their mother's preference for Tony. The mother had always spoken of him as her 'prince'. In fact, Tony had 'believed' her story for many years: he was a real prince who had been given to her by the Royal Family. Of course, far from feeling great (as he was meant to) Tony felt weird, never comfortable in himself. Although he was very intelligent, he had not done well at school; always an outsider, he was unable to make many friends. He was perpetually teased by other kids, and became excruciatingly self-conscious.

After his sister left home, Tony felt claustrophobic living with his mother. He was convinced that she wanted to have an actual incestuous relationship; he was terrified of his mother getting into bed with him at night; he felt utter disgust when she was near him, and yet was afraid of having an erection if his mother physically approached him. All these feelings became unbearable and he finally ran away from home. He lived as a squatter with other young people in a house owned by the then Greater London Council. He lived on unemployment benefits; from time to time, he accepted some financial help from his mother. Tony was quite musical and for many years, while living as a dropout, he wanted to form a small rock'n'roll band. This was one of his few dreams, a project for the future.

During the first 18 months of treatment, a heavy and greatly charged silence dominated our meetings. Tony sat in front of me, eyes shut, saying nothing, maintaining an intense expression on his face. From time to time he mumbled a few words, or would grumble and moan. Sometimes it was more a noise rather than a word that would come out of his mouth. The sessions left me in a dispirited and troubled mood; his misery made me feel hopeless. My efforts to establish a dialogue were mostly met with a silent stony wall. Tony seemed to be living in a truly borderline state, where the limits between his own self and the outer world were blurred. He was also in a hallucinatory state; the only way for him to maintain a certain sense of reality was to keep himself and the world immobile. To think something was to make it reality. All 'bad' thoughts were terribly dangerous: murder and incest, homosexuality and madness were all too close to becoming realised. To talk about them, to pronounce these words was absolutely equivalent to turning them into realities. Thus, Tony kept silent.

Life was a burden, libidinal drives were just too complicated; desires became persecutory. They evoked open landscapes full of dangers; they made Tony feel at sea; he wanted rigid walls around him so as to feel safe. To the outside world he appeared 'dead', as if living in an empty world. However, he established a very passionate, immediate, positive transference relationship with me, which was shown at the beginning, for example, by an intense reaction to arriving late for his sessions. On those occasions he became very upset, beside himself with anger and frustration. Tony had to travel far to get to my consulting room. He depended on the vicissitudes of public transport, and had to combine catching buses with the underground; he had to time his journey very carefully. Nevertheless, Tony was unable to express the frustration or the anger he experienced through being late. If I made a reference to his rage, he took it as a suggestion to put his murderous feelings into action; he reacted with great anxiety and became confused. The same would apply to his feelings of attachment to me in the therapy, which, if interpreted, became the equivalent of a homosexual seduction. At other times, interpretations created a kind of short circuit in his mind; he refused to hear what I had to say, believing that I wanted to force my way into him. Tony experienced my interpretations as 'doing' something to him; he could easily feel invaded by them (in which case he felt that I was poisoning him) or taken over (like a flood of good milk which drowned him).

As reported by authors who have analysed psychotic patients, Tony took my interpretations in a very concrete way. Hanna Segal has described the difficulties of schizophrenic patients to form symbols or to use them; if one interprets castration anxiety, let us say, the interpretation itself could be experienced by the patient as an actual act of castration (Segal 1950, 1957). Nevertheless, in contrast to Segal's description, Tony did not seem to have difficulties with the formation of symbols, nor did he have a serious inhibition about using them. In his case, the confusion between reality and its symbolic representations appeared to have taken place in the area of the self; in other words, Tony's confusion in understanding my interpretations was a consequence of the loss of boundaries between self and others (see Rosenfeld 1952).

The difficulties presented in schizophrenic patients who cannot form or use symbols, as well as the problems presented by patients (like Tony) who experience temporary or chronic loss of boundaries between self and others, should both be distinguished from the symbolically impoverished patients. The latter also confuse what is symbol and what is action, though their sense of self is not as seriously disturbed, making it possible for them to 'function' in the world. For example, they do not experience themselves as possessing a body and a mind with no boundaries; they might appear 'connected' to reality and have fairly 'normal' relationships. Nevertheless, they experience these relationships as a series of actions: one is permanently 'doing' something to something else, and vice versa. The symbolically impoverished patient feels hated by everybody, and this is at the core of their predicament; as a result, words addressed to him might be interpreted as acts of hatred requiring a defensive, hating response. Misunderstanding the analyst's interpretations becomes the central difficulty in the analysis of the symbolically impoverished patients. They are able to experience hate of others (or feel the other's hate) but suffer from a failure to love (Kohon 1999).

While silence prevailed during the initial part of the treatment, this did not mean that the sessions were empty. Tony was under the spell of a much idealised, positive (perhaps even magical) transference, which was easily threatened by his paranoid anxieties. He made me sharply aware of how little it took for me, as his analyst, to become a dangerous and persecuting figure. I too found myself in a very intense relationship with him. For example, I lived in fear that he might do something destructive, either to himself or to others. I would feel (though I never acted on these or similar feelings) a sudden urge to ring him between sessions. I had dreams about him, which showed my own hopelessness and despair in treating him. In one of these dreams, in which I thought he had killed somebody, Tony was asking me compellingly, 'Do you pray? Do you pray for me?'

Possibly, such thoughts and dreams reflected communications coming from Tony, but they did not make me feel invaded, nor did I mind having them. They were a *benign form of projective identification*.[1] What distinguishes this from a *malignant form of projective identification* is that although one finds oneself playing a part in somebody else's fantasy, one does not necessarily feel controlled from within. In other words, these two different forms can be assessed by considering their effect on the recipient subject. In the malignant, pathological form, the recipient of the projection feels the need to push the feelings back where they came from; that is, the feelings projected by the subject are felt as unwelcome by the other. In the benign form, the other person can contain the induced feelings without experiencing loss of freedom. This is similar to the distinction made by Bion between normal and abnormal psychotic projective identification, which is based on the degree of violence of the splitting, the force of the intrusion into the object and the intensity of the hatred directed at it (Bion 1959, 1962). But the terms *benign* and *malignant* allow for the possibility of both forms to co-exist in either neurotic or psychotic individuals. This distinction can also incorporate the difference between projective identification for defensive purposes from the same mechanism when it is used for communication (Rosenfeld 1983). A malignant projective identification, for example, might not necessarily be solely used for defensive purposes; it could be used as a way of communicating unbearable experiences to the object. The character of projective identifications can also change value: what might be malignant at one stage can be processed, worked through, and turned into a benign form at another. During the process of analysis, under certain circumstances of severe stress, a benign form can also turn into a malignant, intrusive projective identification. Occasionally, I used these experiences for my interpretations. I might suggest, for example, that he desperately wanted me to think about him over the weekend, that I should miss him as much as he missed me, that I should not allowed any separation between us to exist. It was vital for Tony that I held him in my mind between sessions; it was something he himself was unable to do with me. On occasion, he was assaulted by doubts about my existence and was tremendously relieved to see me at the next session. The omnipotent idealisation of his relationship with me, and his psychotic perception of me as his saviour and personal messiah, made it difficult for him to believe that I really existed, that I was not just a figment of his imagination.

Tony had frequent visual, olfactory and auditory hallucinations, which persisted (with different intensity) over the first year of treatment. His visual hallucinations were usually connected to objects in the room: the telephone in the corner of my office became a nasty monkey ready to pounce on him. Upon entering the room, he might have the experience of not recognising me. He would think he heard voices: somebody was whispering awful threats into his ear; Tony believed that the voices came through the opening in the fireplace or through the wall from the house next door. He insisted that I should feed him with the supposedly exotic food that he imagined somebody was cooking in the kitchen of my house.

Throughout these difficult times, I was encouraged by the fact that Tony did not act out in any major way. This was a source of great relief for me; it made the intensity and the frustration of my involvement with him bearable. Through his silence he was able to convey his gratitude. In not acting out, he was effectively looking after me and protecting our relationship.

In time, Tony proved to me that he did not lack words: in sharp contrast to the silence of the initial sessions, toward the end of the second year of analysis, he began to write letters. This is part of the text of the first letter:

> Dear Gregsie, Your fucking therapy is no good at all you cunt. It doesnt work . . . I want to kill people I mean kill someone I

> may kill someone literally take a fucking knife and stab some cunt . . . I want drugs LSD I want LSD now I want to go fucking crazy I need heroin I hurt . . . I no longer have any sexual desire thats not funny I want to kill women . . . Tie the fucking bitches up fuck'em in the arse and stab the cunts fuck their wounds and you too cunt you fucker . . . Im gonna fucking smash myself to bits I want to break myself up kill my fucking self . . . I just ate me dinner of the plate like a dog. So I'm back all full up and farting so I'm not angry anymore . . . What a cunt why do I have to come up there eh Why don't you come here. I don't want to earn any money . . . I'm a lot better now thanks doctor. Your office stinks of shit what sort of office is it a shite hole . . . This isn't funny . . . I want 24hr recovery service my bodys all locked up . . . A nice little explanation I want to be a star a fucking star I'm going to be a star.[2]

Tony gave me this letter, scribbled on pages from a notebook, with an uncertain look on his face. I asked him whether he wanted me to read it there and then; he shrugged his shoulders. I decided to do so. He then asked me to keep it, and I agreed. Though I did not explicitly say this then, I considered his writing me a letter a step forward in our relationship; it was a definite progress, compared to communicating with me exclusively through projective identification. There was plenty of material for me to interpret but, initially, spontaneously, I only said, 'It's tough luck you cannot be a fucking star.' He looked at me, rather surprised; this encouraged me. I added a comment about his reference to the money: I said that I realised the uncertainty he was now facing, having to find funds to pay for his therapy. I said that he certainly would never get 24-hr recovery service, but that it would be a great loss if he could not even have the time of his sessions. He gave me a faint, painful smile. Then he broke down and burst into tears. For the rest of that session, we remained in silence. In the following session, he produced another letter:

> I don't care if I' conjuring up your presence. Wouldnt you? Schizophrenia isn't all laughs. There comes a time for a Normalization Process. Cat frying pans.

Letter to My Friends + Family
It's you fault you cunts . . . Mother mostly it's your fault. You made me hate myself so much I cant stand my own mind. Thats why I'm filthy to keep you all away from the shit you made me experience myself as . . . feeling my rage at your screwed up little mind . . . If I'm clean you like me if you like me I feel good but . . . there's a terrible terrible danger of love desire getting in I don't like that . . . panic persecution. Take Vitamin B3 . . . I'm taking off. I feel about as light as a balloon I'm taking off I can't write anymore I'm going onto the ceiling I got a pair of your knickers on Mama. What d'you think of that and I got a pair of Daddys pissed stained pants on. I got'em underneath my hat . . . Seeing flashing lights? Peoples faces changing? Been seing a shrink for years without any change? Take Vitamin B3. I hate you . . .

I told Tony that he desperately wanted to be close to me but was afraid of either my 'totally' rejecting him or my liking him 'too much'. He was still refusing to wash and be clean, and in that way he pushed away any possibility of physical contact with anybody; he was also challenging me to accept him as he was, with all his 'shit'. Wanting to be close to me produced in him feelings of panic and persecution. He wished he could just take something like vitamin B3 and forget about everything; since he could not do that, he 'took off' instead.

During this period in the treatment, Tony communicated with me mainly through these letters: sometimes very long ones, sometimes several in one session. He handed them over to me and closed his eyes. I usually read them straight away, at the time he gave them to me. On occasions, I only read fragments of them or postponed reading them until later in the session. He still refused to speak. Perhaps this was not such an unwise decision; otherwise, the delusional discourse that appeared in his letters would have been made explicit. He could not trust me enough yet. To write the words, instead of speaking them, created a transitional space that could be used by both of us. The emotional impact of the communication was mediated by the act of writing, by the paper, by the silenced words. Tony kept me safe from his delusional attacks, while protecting himself from the possible re-enactment of an invasive mother who did not allow any privacy. Tony's states of mind oscillated between psychotic and non-psychotic periods, but most of the time these two parts of himself seemed to co-exist side by side. Even during the intensely psychotic periods, he did not seem to deny reality. In the psychotic patient whose denial of reality is successful, one could assume that there is no room for fantasies or dreams; the psychic space is colonised by hallucinations. In fact, the appearance of dreams might be a sign of progress in the treatment, of reality becoming more acceptable. Nevertheless, Tony seemed to have fantasies, and he also had dreams; he just did not report them. This is another letter from that period:

> I'm writing under the gaze of your fucking stupid all knowing cunt psychiatrist eye . . . You are the most beautiful woman I have ever met . . . We will go down to the sea. You+I . . . An exploding sunrise I will lick you cock and lie gazing as the sky. All the love in the world will pass between us. We will dissolve into the sky. Carnage+butchery I bear within my soul . . . I want you to be my best friend no I don't . . . Its like I'm hitting an iron door with a feather. I want to scream but I can't in your room . . . I can't say how much I hate you you don't exist you mean nothing to me . . . You are like glue your prick is made of glue I masturbate I really masturbate spunk flows into towels onto floors bits of lavatory paper sheets I covered my sheets in spunk it dried hard I used to wonder what my mother thought I'll send it to you for Christmas The world is dead . . . I will tie you up and shit on you If you start saying 'You want to do this because . . . Youre telling me this because . . .' then I will kill someone . . . You must let me be your son Can this boy survive three days without his therapist?

It was difficult for Tony to experience me as a stable good object. I was not even experienced by him as having the stability of a bad, persecuting object. In his experience, I simply changed from one to the other without any continuity. I could easily move from being an all-knowing cunt [male] psychiatrist to the most beautiful woman;

from his best friend to his most dangerous enemy; from a deaf therapist to a sticky prick or an idealised father. Nevertheless, he used the experience of writing these letters as an attempt at reparation and self-healing; it was a great relief when I had something to say about them, when he felt I had understood. Last, I quote a fragment of another of his letters:

> You are my father. I am the demented child. You have brought me into the world last Christmas . . . If I come here in the middle of the night Why do you care? Do you care? Who are you? Explain. I'm in the room now you're reading the letter . . . Do you accept my foot? Accept my love before I die . . . I don't know when I'm being persecuted by my mother. I'm splitting up. Heat on my neck. Marlene Dietrich on a bad trip. I know why I'm angry. I don't see you often enough. All this is berserk. I'm pretty berserk.

By then, he no longer seemed to be lost in his psychosis. When he wrote 'You are my father', for example, he knew this was impossible; yet, at the same time, this was not the mere expression of a wish. It was more like a concrete and immediate demand that could not, and should not, be refused. It became essential for me to understand, for example, that I could not speak of 'his wish to be my son'. It was much more relevant to let him know that he could not be my son because I did not want it. The direct introduction of my own desire in this way created a necessary third term, an active agency that could not be denied or ignored, shattering the mirage of an imaginary unity between Tony and an idealised mother-imago. For Tony, this was a source of incredible pain and frustration; little by little, he came to accept that this pain was far preferable to the delusional satisfaction of his wishes. The fact that he could stand the pain progressively became a source of strength.

The reference to the foot in the letter was not arbitrary. Sometimes he would take off his shoes to sit in a yoga position on the floor, or lie down on the couch. The stench would almost drive me from the room. For a long time, no interpretation or direct intervention on my part changed his attitude about washing himself. The foot, like other body parts, was something experienced as alien to himself, as a 'real' part that did not connect to him. I interpreted this state of bodily defusion as having originated in the context of an early non-loving relationship with his mother, who had been unable to invest the body of her baby with loving feelings. I told him as much, adding that he could not imagine me, or anybody else for that matter caring for him in a loving way.

Tony experienced his body in bits and pieces; as a way of dealing with this he wished to merge with me in a total, agglutinated and amorphous unity. In some sessions, Tony would be fixed on part of his body, looking at his knee, for example, or his hand. The same might happen with a picture on the wall of my consulting room. He would then find it difficult to 'move on' to other things because he lost the original connection with the context in which these things existed. The links that we normally take for granted were missing in his mind: a hand was a hand, separated from the rest of his body; thus, it had no meaning. He would ask: 'What is a hand for?' This was not a rhetorical or philosophical question. Any part of his body could potentially turn into a persecuting object. By concentrating his attention on one element, Tony's perceptual Gestalt was lost. It could help to think of this in terms of the narrative of a film that was disjointed. *Raccords* (correspondences) are what make syntactic continuity possible from frame to frame in a film sequence: they heal the gaps in the narrative, avoiding unwelcome *coupures* (confusing cuts). Tony appeared to perceive the world like a movie where the *raccords* were missing; this was reflected in the way his thought processes were constructed and expressed.

For a very long time in the analysis, Tony was not able to look at me, nor could he look at the things in my consulting room. If he did look at me, he felt that the distance between him and me would completely disappear. He felt that he could, if he wished, penetrate me with his gaze and destroy me. He imagined that I might want to do the same to him. Perception did not respect the object's integrity; the boundaries between subject and objects, and between objects themselves could not be kept. Confusion and angst contaminated all perceptual experiences. In fact, every object perceived, or any apparently arbitrary or minute aspect of the object, could become for him too special, all important, all encompassing. His perception could transform a small event into an enormously far-reaching, meaningful moment. Tony kept his eyes closed, his mouth shut, his ears blocked, but reality always managed to impinge on him. To allow reality to be perceived reminded him of the strangeness of things, of his own sense of dislocation and displacement. What could he do but keep himself paralysed, and the world at a distance? Tony presented many characteristics found in schizophrenic patients. For example, his catatonic posture at the beginning of the analysis was dominated by the classically described hyperconsciousness of these patients, which makes all forms of introspection painfully focused. The pseudo-detachment offered by his physical rigidity gave Tony a peculiar sense of power, as if standing back from experience could make him feel that the whole world depended on him. He, and only he, wished to give existence to the world outside and to the objects that existed in that world. Concerned at times with the very existence of the world, there was no apparent room or time in his life to be involved with more mundane things: jobs, career, normal sadness, the burden of everyday life.

In the treatment, writing letters confirmed his way of denying the separation between us; he pulled me out of my own, private environment and forced me into his. His negativism was at work: refusing to talk had been a rejection of the terms I had put forward for the analysis. I did not mind, even when I had found his long silences and his despair very difficult. But it soon became clear that the experience of writing letters had been essential for the continuation of the treatment. He had been literally terrified of saying whatever came to his mind. For him, it was no effort to free associate. Writing down his thoughts, frustrating as it was, offered him a certain sense of control. Talking to me, as much as looking at me, were sources of great terror, for he felt that the boundaries between us would disappear.

Tony, in his omnipotence, felt superior to others, pleased with himself for being 'different'; in many ways, he expected my admiration for being 'better' than his 'normal' mother and sister. And yet, he had little reason to feel proud of himself. He knew he was psychotic, felt completely lost in life, and experienced as a dangerous threat his intense wishes to kill himself and others. It took him some time to admit it, but he also felt profoundly ashamed of his madness.

There was a third period of Tony's therapy, based almost exclusively on the analysis of his dreams. The move from writing letters to telling me dreams represented a natural step in the development of his therapy. To tell me his dreams took more courage than writing; it was an invitation for me to share more of his internal world. Tony became capable of separating from the external objects that subjugated him in reality. It helped him to establish a sense of separateness that, even though extremely precarious, made him feel alive. Literally, this meant that he was capable of having a mind of his own. I was amazed to see how he started to be capable of contemplating thinking as an independent, exclusive and playful activity. This was not easily achieved: as soon as he caught himself enjoying his thoughts, Tony feared that his mother would discover them and read them. Nevertheless, he felt more hopeful; he could dare to defy an angry, jealous, paranoid mother, who (in his experience) had kept a tight control over his mind throughout his life. Now, he felt that he could have his thoughts without somebody else guessing them. The capacity to have thoughts and to be able to hide them was the first step towards true emotional independence. Tony discovered that he could have his own secrets, which meant that he could lie (like anybody else in this world) as well as tell the truth. This activity gave him enormous pleasure: it was like seeing a child with a new toy. The fact that he could think of the pleasure present in the activity of thinking made a large contribution to his recovery. One particular dream illustrated this movement:

> He was travelling on a train with an old woman, a stranger, who kept complaining about everything: the seating arrangements, the food, the temperature of the carriage. He did not know why but he felt embarrassed, as if he were responsible for her. Everybody was looking; he felt more and more uncomfortable. He wanted to push her out of the train but realised that it was none of his business. Finally, the woman descended at a station. It was near the Botanical Gardens at Kew, close to his mother's house. He then realised he was on his way to a session.

He was especially pleased that he had not pushed his mother out of the train in the dream. He had felt murderous towards her so many times in the past, it was a relief to not have to experience the persecuting guilt those feelings had always provoked in him. The reference to the botanical gardens was perhaps the most important signifier in the dream. In a recent session, Tony had made fun of Prince Charles and of the Prince's alleged habit of 'talking to plants'. So now Tony had felt that he was leaving his mother's 'prince' behind, with her, while he was travelling along, away from his mother, towards his analytic session.

As he began to feel less paranoid, he started to do some work; his first job was cleaning private houses, through an agency. Given his own problems with cleanliness, this was a real laugh. We discovered that we could share the humour in these things. In fact, irony and laughter then became important elements of the therapeutic relationship. I believe that had this not happened, had we not been able to laugh together, Tony's analysis would have proved impossible.

The saner Tony became, the crazier his mother and sister looked. The relationship between Tony and his sister had always been based on anger, competition, jealousy and rivalry; now, the difference was that Tony seemed to be able to defend himself more effectively. In one of the fights he reported, his sister started punching him, shouting, 'You're psychotic! You're psychotic!' At this point, Tony was definitely not psychotic. He said in that session, 'Now I know that my madness is their madness; they can have it back.' His sister's frustration at not being able to 'win' the argument by intimidating Tony, as previously, made her wish that 'things could be like they used to be'.

As I mentioned at the beginning, his mother had originally agreed to pay for Tony's therapy for one year, extended thereafter to a second. After that, Tony managed to pay for his own treatment. I agreed to keep my fees low until he was able to earn his living; this lasted for many years, after which he paid my regular fee. Tony's mother seemed to find his growing independence very difficult: she tried to undermine his therapy and interfere in his relationship with me. For example, she would make ironic comments about his therapist, or sarcastic remarks about the progress of the therapy. Tony felt caught up in the conflict; he thought his mother was trying to seduce him away from me; he felt guilty towards both his mother and me; his mother accused me of 'taking her boy away', of turning her into a bad mother. At one point, during the sixth year of therapy, she sent the following poem to him:

> A SONG FOR MY SON/Let you concern yourselves with my son/For he is mad./He stands apart and out of his eyes fall/ Suns and starts. Galaxies/Pour through his veins, but blood is on his lips/His life bleeds from his lips./His cries shriek out from The Abyss/He yearns to be again/Nothing and All,/The stuff of Creation before the first Sun/Frenzied Nothing with Fire . . ./You raise you dry eyes/Laugh at the riding boy of unreason/And your laugh is loud and terrible/More sad than your tears of the wandering, riding madman . . . /He r{e}aches my hands in headlong his high fight/Shrieking ecstasies 'Come drink my blood of Light/Drink and be mad with ecstasies of fire/Of winds of water – lightning and the howling sea'/His blinding light unblinds my blindness/One moment. Oh almost I reach the flaming hands/Almost ride the airless furnace of the Void/with the Boy of madness and truth/Know flow through my fingers the sand of the stars/When my son's tears fall over unborn constellations . . .

The impact of this poem on Tony was staggering; it provoked one of the most regressive reactions of his analysis. It made him feel that whatever progress he had made, he was not going to be able to change his relationship with his mother; something in him was going to stay mad forever. Furthermore, he was thrown back into a confused state and could not discriminate which madness belonged to whom. He was convinced that he had driven his mother crazy; this terrified him: his own madness could drive me crazy. He wanted to stop the treatment; he claimed that it was all a waste of time and money. He became paranoid again and thought people were following him around underground stations; he felt ill and physically weak. He imagined raping his mother at his sister's place, of biting her tongue out while kissing her on the mouth. He became intensely jealous of anybody who approached or talked to his new girlfriend; he was convinced that because of his regression she was going to leave him. He could not bear the presence of any other patient in the waiting room; he was aggressive and nasty to other people when crossing them on the stairs. He could not distinguish whether he was having all these 'bad' feelings because of his own problems, or because – he suggested – he was becoming his mother. He seriously thought of killing her. In one session, he reverted to writing letters:

> I can't talk but I keep thinking things like your mother wouldn't like it if you didn't care for her I wouldn't like it if she didn't care for me I can't get it in my head it's terrifying I can't believe my mother hates me or I hate her. Remember I'm not a vicious man. I'm not bad. Yet he was hitting me he did hate me now you know what it felt like when your father saw you with your mother . . . They wouldn't admit they were wrong Somewhere they're such a lie fucking hell I'm in hell . . . My father is dead because I didn't help him in the garden. My mother said: 'I remember a few days before he died working so hard in the garden – and you wouldn't help him'. I killed my old man, anyone who kills their old man is a bastard . . . I just cut myself this is my blood [there were in fact dried bloodstains on the paper] I was thinking of suicide . . . That word SPLIT is dead right I'm writing to stay alive You inhuman charlatan I'm warning you This letter reminds me of the beginning when I first knew you . . . You can't even speak English. How the hell can it work when you can't even speak fucking English . . . I need to be able to hate her.

I feared that Tony's severe regression might prompt another breakdown. Nevertheless, the fact that we did have the opportunity to analyse how he felt invaded and driven mad by his mother helped him to get through this period. He realised that his mother was insensitive to his needs, and this – far from being a mere product of his internal world – reflected the reality of the situation. The way in which he split the world into extremes of good and bad was an attempt to keep some sanity in the mother, some belief that she was not as horrible as she seemed. But he had to reconcile himself to the possibility that she might be as bad as he thought she was. He had believed in the past that his mother spoke a strange language, that he could not understand what she said. He was afraid that my deficiencies with the English language were proof of my own insensitivity towards his needs. He also wanted to attack me with something that would really hurt me; he wished he could demean and belittle me.

This regressive episode was yet another reminder of how much he needed me; Tony was ashamed of his psychotic self. His dependence on me, and his passionate (transference) love for me humiliated him; he desperately wanted to make me feel the same way. The intensity of his feelings provoked in me a powerful sense of guilt: I felt I had let Tony down, betrayed him, that I should have been able to protect him from his mother. With patients like Tony, I now believe that the analyst cannot limit his interpretations to the unconscious fantasy of the patient; also required is a specific acknowledgement of the reality of the actual dynamics of the therapeutic encounter. What I mean is that in circumstances like these, it seemed necessary for me to recognise that I was in effect unable to protect Tony, and only then proceed with analytic interpretation. To give an example, it is the difference between saying to a patient 'Perhaps you feel that I cannot protect you from your mother' and saying 'The dilemma is that I cannot protect you from your mother, that I cannot be there with you, which is the only way you believe you would feel protected, that you could survive.' Otherwise, I believe that a psychotic patient could hardly trust the analyst to understand him or her.

The subsequent period of the analysis was fruitful. Tony realised how much he needed to separate from the maternal body in which he had been trapped. As much as he wanted to live in a beatific delusional unity with his mother, psychosis was too high a price to pay. 'My father is dead because I didn't help him in the garden. My mother said . . .' It was the word of the mother, establishing a false order of things: guilt, submission, emotional terrorism, but no real recognition in the mother of a word that belonged to the father. Father had lived in the shadows of his own past: his first marriage had been the subject of innumerable fights between him and Tony's mother; he had no place in the unyielding psychotic bubble that mother and son had formed. Tony had had the delusion that he could be everything for mother, but now he began to discover that this had been his mother's original wish. What had appeared to be an intense Oedipal drama was a deceptive pantomime: Tony could not love his mother because she did not exist for him in any separate way; nor did he exist for his mother. He could not own his own words: it was his mother who had said that he had killed his father. He did not know what place he occupied in a triangle: he was a Royal prince, with no father; he had been given to mother for her own satisfaction. The man who had been known as his father belonged to another family constellation, to the first woman he had married. For Tony, to have the surname of his father did not identify him as his father's son; he felt outside the movement of the generations. He accepted these interpretations.

In the middle of his process of recovery, Tony received yet another long letter from his mother. I will only quote a short fragment:

> DANGER!! Jocasta calling!! If youve got 2 p to spare & an inclination to oblige an old geyser shed much appreciate -If not- forget it. Things arent at all up to mark here at Thebes. The latest trouble is that bloody sphinx. Blatantly neglecting her duties especially in her aspect of destructive Maternal Force. Shes been openly saying 'Who does Zeus think he is anyway lobbering me with such a job in the first place & then underpaying me with all those jobs Ive had to devour because they were too thick to answer a damn silly riddle. They've given me serious stomach trouble . . . [She ended the letter thus:] Given at Thebes BC 1000 or there about a few centuries one way or another/ Jocasta Regina.

Tony could not find any humour in this. Consequently, after a few sessions he felt profoundly sad about his mother, and said to me: 'She is mad but I'm not going to sacrifice myself for her. If she wants to go to Hell, let her, she's going alone. Let her burn, let it be fire.' It was at this point that the nature of the therapeutic work in Tony's analysis truly changed. Still, it took another few years for us to part. During that time he continued to move between a paranoid-schizoid and a depressive mode of being, but he was well aware of his own limitations: how easily, for example, he could become anxious and paranoid. Nevertheless, he was never psychotic again; he no longer experienced delusions, hallucinations or 'thought disorders'.

THE HEROIC ACHIEVEMENT OF SANITY

Given the fact that human beings are born prematurely when compared to other higher mammals, they only survive thanks to the intervention of a physical and psychological environment that will protect them, look after them, feed them, and in general terms help them to develop for a relatively long time. Freud described the human baby as being born in a state of helplessness, an incapacity to help itself. The baby is completely dependent on other people for the satisfaction of its most basic needs. The mother, or the caretaking environment, can be said to fulfil the function, in the outside world, of a protective shield (Khan 1963).

Freud described two types of helplessness at this initial stage in life: motor helplessness, in reference to the specific action that is needed to satisfy a need; and psychical helplessness, the inability of the psychical apparatus to cope with, and control the increase in tension. While in *Beyond the Pleasure Principle* (1920) Freud saw as traumatic 'any situations from outside which are powerful enough to break through the protective shield' (p. 29), in *Inhibitions, Symptoms and Anxiety* (1926), he used the concept of helplessness as the prototype of the traumatic situation.

According to Laplanche and Pontalis, the concept of helplessness 'is at the root of several lines of psycho-analytic inquiry'. From the genetic point of view:

> . . . it is on the basis of this idea that we are able to understand the primordial role played by the experience of satisfaction, its hallucinatory reproduction and the distinction between the primary and secondary processes.
> (Laplanche and Pontalis 1967: 190)

The importance of this first experience of satisfaction (which will determine all future experiences of pleasure) resides in the fact that the hallucinatory process does not deny reality. Just the opposite, it helps to recognise the existence of a reality outside the self, different from it, which needs to be found. The hallucinatory process helps to recognise such a thing as a breast, existing in the world as part of a mother. More than anything else, it shows the baby's wish to take possession of the breast inside his mouth.

The second important line of inquiry is that (given the total dependence of the human infant on its environment) 'the state of helplessness [of the baby] implies the mother's omnipotence' – somebody has to be omnipotent to save the baby from total destruction (Laplanche and Pontalis 1967: 190). How could she not be omnipotent? First, she is the one who has given birth to the baby; then, she makes it possible for him to survive, and finally, she is the provider of the original experiences of safety and of pleasure. This omnipotent mother, who can do anything, does not need anybody else. The fixation on this relationship with a primary object, in the initial phase of an exclusive as well as intense lasting attachment, will be the source of psychotic states and the perversions. And at the origin of all forms of love.

The inevitable discrepancy between the baby's helplessness and the mother's omnipotence prepares the ground for the possibility of primary violence:

> The mother's discourse [. . .] is the agent responsible for the effect of anticipation imposed on the infant, from whom a response is expected that it is not in his power to give . . .
> (Aulagnier 1975: 11)

Physical dependence on others for survival goes hand in hand with emotional immaturity; babies are at the mercy of potentially overwhelming anxieties and frustrations. The mother imposes her desire on the baby, for example, by offering and pushing her nipple into his mouth. This could, in certain circumstances, reinforce the sense of helplessness in the baby. This is indeed a passivation of the baby by the mother (as described by Green 1980): the baby has to submit to the care provided by the mother; he needs to trust that the mother will not take advantage of his vulnerability, that she will not misunderstand his 'language'. But, as Freud, Winnicott, Klein and others have shown, the baby is far from passive. Melanie Klein has given us a description of unsurpassed insight of the baby's active searching, not so much for an object, but for what could be defined as the pleasure of the object (Green 2002). The breast is the infant's first object of desire; the mother, the first object of love. The physical relationship with mother (nursing, touching, being cuddled and caressed) necessarily includes sexual and erotic feelings. Melanie Klein stated it thus:

> I would not assume that the breast is [to the baby] merely a physical object. The whole of his instinctual desires and his unconscious phantasies imbue the breast with qualities going far beyond the actual nourishment it affords.
>
> (Klein 1957: 180)

It is not only the baby who invests the breast with such qualities and wishes. From the beginning of life it takes at least two to tango: what is on offer is not just milk; it also includes the mother's own instinctual desires and unconscious fantasies. In this encounter between the unconscious of mother and baby, the breast is a libidinal object for both participants; the dynamics of give and take are multidimensional and overdetermined. The baby is confronted with the task of metabolising something which never arrives as always the same; he will never know quite what he is getting next time round. Warm milk, cold milk, milk that tastes sour, poisonous milk, milk too rich to be comfortably digested, milk received from an eroticised breast. Milk that gives pleasure; the same milk, inaugurating a life of unpleasure. Not just milk then, not just simple nourishment to help him survive; it is a rather complex emotional package to be unwrapped and metabolised. So, here it is: the first mouthful of meaning that the baby will receive. Love and hate. The scene in which the drama of love is staged originates in need; at this point, the fear of the loss of love is equivalent to the fear of not being able to survive.

While the stage of dependence lasts for a long time, this prolonged period creates the conditions for a fruitful process of learning. Right from the first experience of feeding, some sort of pattern will be established; if the experiences are frequent and good enough, there will a representation of 'the breast'. The baby will be able to desire (represent) the breast that he needs for his survival. Whenever the breast (re-)appears, fulfilling the desire of the subject, love is possible. Nevertheless, the good breast is never just good: the appearance itself of desire denotes the absence of what is missing. The relationship with the breast entails the ongoing process of comings and goings, of the mother's presence and absence. With each absence (if it is not too prolonged) the desire for her presence is established more clearly.

The search for an object in the real world is entirely governed by a relationship to signs. The dynamics of the *Fort-Da,* through the symbolic representation of the presence and absence of the mother, portrays the mythical moment of the acquisition of language. The unconscious might not be structured like a language (as Lacan wished it were), but language plays a fundamental and decisive part in the establishment and structuring of the baby's subjectivity. From the beginning of life, the subject relates to other subjects. Even before the infant can understand language, before he has developed his capacity for linguistic expression (one could argue, even before his birth), he lives in a cultural milieu, which provides a context and extensive references to his existence. We are conceived, born, and exist in a world of others; it is these relationships that give meaning to our lives.[3] These subjects are desiring subjects, who impose their own linguistic code on the newly arrived. The baby arrives to a meaningful world, marked and defined by language. The baby is born in a human world of enigmatic signifiers (Laplanche 1987), which are alien to him. There is an unconscious process of *implantation* of enigmatic verbal and non-verbal messages in the primitive body-ego of the infant – messages derived from the adults' sexuality. Laplanche describes this as the *fundamental anthropological situation* of the human infant. Being enigmatic, these signifiers are the source of innumerable misunderstandings. The baby falls into a world of significant others: mother, father, grandparents, with their own desires and their histories, their dreams and their own personal myths. The baby is to discover that, prior to his birth, he has been existing in the mind of others; he has been given a name, has become part of a myth determined by others' desires. The world that welcomes him belongs to others; there will always be a considerable *plus* of signification that the baby will not be able to decode. In a scene described by A. S. Byatt in her novel *Still Life*, a mother is talking to her newborn son:

> She had not expected ecstasy. She noted that he was both much more solid, and, in the feebleness of his fluttering movements of lip and cheek muscle, the dangerous lolling of his uncontrolled head, more fragile, than she had expected . . . She put out a finger and touched [his] fist; he obeyed a primitive instinct and curled the tiny fingers round her own, where they clutched, loosened, tightened again. 'There,' she said to him, and he looked, and the light poured through the window, brighter and brighter, and his eyes saw it, and hers, and she was aware of bliss, a word she didn't like, the only one. There was her body, quiet, used, resting; there was her mind, free, clear, shining; there was the boy and his eyes, seeing what? And ecstasy. Things would hurt when this light dimmed. The boy would change. But now in the sun she recognised him, and recognised that she did not know, and had never seen him, and loved him, in the bright new air with a simplicity she had never expected to know. 'You,' she said to him, skin for the first time on skin in the outside air, which was warm and shining, 'you'.
>
> (Byatt 1985: 100–101, quoted in Muller 1996)

The mother gives meaning to the baby's experiences, a meaning that the baby cannot yet create or have by himself. The mother anticipates what the baby is due to discover. When the mother speaks, she inaugurates a dialogue, an exchange between herself and her baby, which is unique and fundamental. While the mother uses language, mother and baby operate within a proto-linguistic system (Bruner 1990), communicating with each other. The constitution of the baby's subjectivity is realised through a series of consecutive and dialectical representations and misrepresentations of this original primary scenario in which mother and baby interact. It is these words, *there, you,* as we imagine them being spoken with love by the mother, that make the subjectivity of the baby possible. *You,* says she, the giver of meaning, provider of goodness, source of contentment. How does the baby interpret this declaration of love? The word of the mother, if spoken with pleasure, will create pleasure. If uttered with love, it will be assimilated as part of the self and generate love. But if the word is not there, or the voice is hateful, uncertain or troubled by too much ambivalence, if it is misleading or deceitful, then the baby responds with confusion, insecurity and a sense of loss. The word of the significant other will remain in this case an alien object, a separate internal object which will become persecuting, attacking the creative possibilities of integration and links. Pleasure will be replaced by uncertainty; love, substituted by fear. Excessive love, or exclusive love offered by an omnipotent giver will determine an anxious response. 'I'm my mother's fantasy,' Tony used to say.

This has been described in Lacan's reformulation of the mirror stage in his *Seminars* (1960–61). In his revised view, the image offered by the mirror is internalised and libidinally invested by the infant (thus, confirming the child's existence as a whole) because the parent, holding the child up to the mirror, offers a (verbal) gesture of approval. We have a significant scenario here: the parent's recognition of the child in the mirror is what becomes truly important. The child is not, after all, the one celebrating on his own the discovery of his specular image in a mythical moment of narcissistic jubilation (as originally described by Lacan, 1936 [1949]). It is the parent, or parental figures saying (signifying) 'you, you, that is you', who offer the necessary recognition and acknowledgement. The other-than-himself of the mirror is pulled away, forced either to look at the mother, or – at least – listen to the mother. The intervention of a linguistic code establishes the presence of a third term, right from birth.

For different theoretical reasons, Lacan – as well as Melanie Klein – both postulated a precocious Oedipus complex. Lacan called it *le toujours-déjà-là,* the always-already-there of the complex. There is no pre-Oedipal without an Oedipal structure; in fact, that is why it is called pre-Oedipal; the Oedipal is there, if only as a negative reference. If sight were the only origin of subjectivity, the subject would then be trapped in a narcissistic predicament. But the word of the mother introduces a break in the process of primary identification of the baby with his narcissistic image in the mirror. The words of this pre-Oedipal mother represent the confirmation that she constitutes herself as a primitive third term in the baby's mind. This is a true dialectical moment: the recognition of the subjectivity of the baby (through the signifying utterances of the mother) denotes, implies simultaneous recognition of her own subjectivity.

As soon as the baby is imagined (inside the womb), named, talked about, feared, or idealised, the baby–mother dyad contains a third term as a reference. The progressive development of these subjectivities and their mutual recognition reduces the mother's omnipotence and the baby's need to use extreme defences. It inaugurates an inter-subjective space, a transitional space which is at the core of the process of symbolisation.

The two aspects of the original state of helplessness (the hallucinatory experience of satisfaction on one hand and the omnipotence of the mother on the other) create the conditions for a *normal madness* to develop. This madness is only tempered by the presence of a third term (in the mind of the mother). This is the time when what will be on offer to the baby dangerously borders on excess: presence and absence, love and hate, attention and indifference, closeness and distance, physical contact and avoidance – all of this can be too much. Or too soon. Or too little. Or too late. In fact, this normal madness is none other than the world of internal objects as described by Melanie Klein: primitive fears and terrors, and intense and extreme anxieties. In her early view, initial object relations were shaped by very sadistic fantasies. In her mature view, she understood the earliest fantasy life of the infant in terms of equally extremes of love and hate in which very good and very bad objects co-existed and had to be kept apart. Klein's compelling description of the baby's internal world does not exclude exposure to a natural, unavoidable, and yet potentially traumatic imposition from the outside.

André Green called this situation 'original madness' ('maternal madness' in the French version) (Green 1980; see also Eigen 1999). It is indeed original: it takes place at the origins of normal individual human development, at the peak of intense primitive psychic activity. It is also original in the sense of its uniqueness;

it represents something 'absolutely personal' for the individual, being at the core of who he is (Winnicott 1989). It is the personal madness present later in all forms of love, clearly visible in (transference-) love. It is there in all manifestations of the drives, in every expression of sexuality; it is the madness of pleasure and desire, of narcissism and idealisation, a basic madness which informs human life right from the start. I would prefer to call it normal, in Winnicott's sense: 'Normal is what is there,' he said (1989: 270). The baby does not know anything else; the use of extreme primary defences at the onset of life is nothing but justified. The baby gets what he can, and if he wants to survive (and one can assume that most babies do) then he might have to take whatever he gets, in whatever way he can. If the emotional nourishment on offer is toxic or poisoned, nourishment contaminated by hate, envy, jealousy, etc., then extreme measures and counter-attacks might be necessary, and called upon, to digest it (Eigen 1999). It makes perfect 'normal' sense. Thus understood, madness is not an occasional alteration in adult mental life; it is an inevitable component of psychic life throughout the subject's life – as long as he or she is alive, continues to experience emotions, and is capable of passion. First experienced in the initial encounter with mother, it will be at the core of the subject's unconscious. Like the residues of a dream, it will (re) appear, more or less in disguise, in every aspect of the subject's internal life. At the origin, it can be argued, there was madness ... Sanity is a surplus benefit (J. Sekoff, personal communication), not included in the initial bargain of being born. Sanity is the result of a process whereby the use and the impact of primitive defences slowly decreases. Subjectivity and relative neurotic normality appear as genuinely heroic achievements (Eigen 1999).

Early normal madness does not necessarily create psychosis. Green introduced a distinction between madness and psychosis. Madness is not pathological; it is linked to 'the vicissitudes of a primordial Eros' (Green 1980). In fact, this follows the *Oxford English Dictionary*'s definition of these two words. While *psychosis*, in modern times, describes any mental illness accompanied by hallucinations, delusions, mental confusion and/or loss of contact with reality, *madness* is a more inclusive concept – it describes a multiplicity of phenomena, from insanity to rage, anger or violence.

To be mad could cover being stupefied by fear or suffering; being carried away by enthusiasm or desire; infatuated; wildly excited, extravagant (*OED*).

Piera Aulagnier (1975) speaks of a psychotic potentiality in the baby, a madness that in normal circumstances could be contained within the relationship with the mother. Sometimes, such containment fails to happen. In his description of the fundamental anthropological situation of the human infant, Laplanche introduced the concept of *intromission*, a 'violent variant' of the normal process of implantation. In the case of intromission, the message is not allowed to be decoded; the violence of the parents in sending the message actively interferes with the possibility of translation and metabolisation. It is not just that these tasks are difficult by definition, but that the infant is subjected to a malignant process which 'puts into the interior an element resistant to all metabolisation' (Laplanche 1956: 136). Implantation could turn into intromission for a variety of reasons. For example, the existence of unknown constitutional factors might determine a weak primitive body-ego (Freud 1923: 26), which does not provide enough of a protective shield against the messages received. Also, mothering functions might be repeated and prolonged for too long; they might be unduly intense, or emotionally charged in such a way that the actions change their meaning. Unknown and/or unpredicted factors might also contribute to the failure of translation, producing unsuccessful attempts at metabolising signifiers. Finally, another important factor might be the presence of an intense unbound sexuality which permeates and contaminates every action on the part of the adult.[4]

When the mother responds inadequately to the baby's needs, the baby tends to organise his responses in a distorted fashion. From clinical experience we can tentatively conclude that, given certain circumstances, madness develops into proper psychosis whenever a baby (in the thrust of having to cope with his own madness) has to deal with the madness of the primary object as well. If this is too frequent and too intense, it becomes a cumulative trauma (Khan 1963). With each failure in the encounter between mother and baby, progressively a malignant pattern is established. A deluded, depressed, pathologically disturbed mother is not able to contain her baby's projections, anxieties and feelings. Her anxious response to the excesses of love and hate of that primary relationship intensify (rather than minimise) the baby's own responses. In psychosis, what has not been repressed in the parents returns as delusions in the psychosis of their child (Aulagnier 1975). As delusions, they hide what had originally failed to be repressed in the parents, but which by now can no longer be identified properly. At its worst, this might constitute the beginning of a truly delusional process. From the original situation of normal madness, the relationship might develop into a shared love/hate psychosis between mother and baby. Ironically, a psychotic pact might help the mother to sustain an apparent sanity; it acts as scaffolding, which prevents the collapse of the building.

Tony was made to believe, and compelled to interpret the love of his mother as something exclusive. The baby might indeed want to be the exclusive object of maternal love, but to remain fixated to this omnipotent desire is the wish of the psychotic. Tony's mother tried to convince him that her love for him excluded everybody else: no father, no other child (sister) seemed to occupy such a privileged place in his mother's heart. The only object of the mother's desire was Tony. She was interfering and seductive; always demanding, always telling him what to do and how to be, his mother was never absent; he suffered all his life the terror of being taken over and overwhelmed by this powerful maternal object – his own personal 'influencing machine' (Tausk 1919). He was always too excited, anxious, on edge. By turning Tony into a baby desired and created by the Royal Family, the mother's discourse did not include her own desire, nor did she include a father with a desire of his own; there was no father whose desire would take mother away. Unable to cathect the sexual relationship with her husband, Tony's mother related to Tony through a process of idealisation of his origin, effectively, depriving him of his true origin; she could not tell him, 'You are *my* prince.' Thus, a sense of belonging eluded Tony; it did not speak to him: he was alien to his life. The question forced upon each human being by the Oedipus story is not only the triangular tragedy of rivalry, jealousy and love but also the drama of misrecognition (*méconnaissance*) of their own history: Oedipus is the son of Jocasta and Laius but he does not know it. In not being able to recognise his own history, he cannot identify or know his desire. Tony's fantasised origin did not refer to Tony himself; it spoke of his mother's own deluded origin. A father did exist (if only to have been killed in reality by Tony, according to his mother's version), but this man had nothing to do neither with mother's desires, nor with a desire of his own for the mother. The representation offered by the mother of the parents' sexual encounter was not one of mutual desire, but of two desires, mother's and father's, rejecting each other.

Normal madness makes its most dramatic and undeniable (re)appearance in the situation of transference. Strange love, this, the patient's transference-love towards a stranger. Analysis creates the conditions for this love to develop, greatly helped by the intense resistance that announces that the subject prefers to repeat rather than remember. This intriguing piece of real life erupting into the consulting room with uncanny strength cannot be ignored, dismissed or reduced to a compulsion to repeat repressed infantile conflicts. As distressing and comical as the situation of an intense and passionate transference-love may be, it is also *serious* (Freud 1915: 159). Things to do with love (like transference) cannot be compared to any other emotional phenomena: 'they are . . . written on a special page on which no other writing is tolerated' (p. 160). But (transference-)love, this 'spirit of the underworld' which we have summoned up 'by cunning spells' (p. 164), is it real? Is it true? Freud's summary is worth quoting at length:

> We have no right to dispute that the state of being in love which makes its appearance in the course of analytic treatment has the character of a 'genuine' love. If it seems so lacking in normality, this is sufficiently explained by the fact that being in love in ordinary life, outside analysis, is also more similar to abnormal than to normal mental phenomena. Nevertheless, transference-love is characterized by certain features which ensure it a special position. In the first place, it is provoked by the analytic situation; secondly, it is greatly intensified by the resistance, which dominates the situation; and thirdly, it is lacking to a high degree in a regard for reality, is less sensible, less concerned about the consequence and more blind in its

valuation of the loved person than we are prepared to admit in the case of normal love. *We should not forget, however, that these departures from the norm constitute precisely what is essential about being in love.*

(Freud 1915: 168–169, italics added)

As experiences go, transference (always related to an object *in the present*) has an unparalleled immediacy – and yet clinical psychoanalysis cannot be reduced and limited to its interpretation. We are aware that some psychoanalysts suffer the fascination of continuously decoding the content of what is being said by the patient in terms of the transference, creating the illusion of a thorough understanding; they behave as if they believe that 'transference' equals 'the unconscious'. Transference interpretations create a meaning of sorts, but they do not constitute the meaning of all meanings.

Most of the time, in the treatment of psychotic and seriously borderline patients, we are dealing with something unspeakable. If the unconscious were structured like a language, the treatment of these patients would be impossible. Even taking into consideration the uncertainty of these cures, they show that psychoanalysis, though unable to go beyond language, is still quite capable of cutting across it. In most cases, psychotic patients live in a constant state of psychic agony, which is not only unthinkable (Winnicott 1963) but also unnameable. In the analysis, they move from intense separation anxiety to the terror of being intruded upon by the analyst's presence and words. While they develop a passionate attachment to the analyst and to the sessions, the horror of being intruded upon is always threatening the relationship with the analyst. This is at the core of the fear of further breakdowns. How can the analyst help his patient to make this agony bearable?

The main difficulty resides in the patient's central dilemma: on the one hand, he needs the analysis but experiences the psychoanalytic situation itself as a repetition of the original trauma. He might want and need the analyst's words but tries to avoid them; the need itself is experienced as a great humiliation. The analyst, in trying to make sense of the patient's predicament, re-enacts a trauma which perhaps could not even have been experienced in the past, which has thus become frozen (Winnicott 1954). In many cases, the communication to the patient becomes itself traumatic (Kohon 1999). The presence as well as the absence of the analyst is experienced as impingements. Events in life are experienced as impingement when the infant is not able to process what is happening to him (Winnicott 1949 [1954], 1962). Instead of being able to digest the experience, and use it for growth and further development, the infant reacts with panic and terror. A mismatch has occurred between the baby and the environment. Confusion between love and hate ensues; this makes it impossible for the subject to discriminate between good and bad objects. Rosenfeld described patients feeling phobic about their own mothers: they are terrified that they have to defend themselves against something extremely dangerous; for example, the physical experience of being fed becomes confused with being poisoned (Rosenfeld 1987). In analysis, the desire to be recognised by the analyst makes these patients feel vulnerable and eventually confused. To love and be loved comes at a price. But they believe they will lose the precarious sense of reality they have achieved so painfully and are convinced they will have to replace their reality with the analyst's own version of it. Some of these patients do not seem to possess the necessary protective shield which would safeguard them from the outside world.

In psychosis, the confusion between love and hate, the extreme uncertainty about what is good and what is bad for the subject, cause life and death also to be confused. Tony had the omnipotent fantasy of 'paralysing' time in order to eliminate the differences between being alive and being dead. In one session, he said, 'I can't sleep next to Alice [his girlfriend], she feels too hot, I'll get burnt, I feel all cold inside me, my body doesn't exist, I can't shit, I can't fuck, I can't eat . . . to feel is like being torn to pieces, feelings are dangerous, I have nothing to say.' On another occasion, he declared, 'I want to retreat from life, to live is too dangerous for me, I'd like everything to be dead . . . when I walk down the streets, everything is still, like ice, I feel dead, I never left my mother's womb.'

This confusion between birth and death seems to be particularly evident in most forms of psychotic thinking, especially in the case of genuinely schizophrenic patients (Kohon 1976). Mr R had been a psychiatric patient for a while before coming to see me for treatment; he was living in a private therapeutic community while he attended analysis with me. On several occasions he had to be hospitalised and I visited him in hospital for his sessions. He was, despite his illness, incredibly resourceful, but could not put this to good use. For example, Mr R once managed to get through several security checkpoints at the American embassy – even then, in the early 1970s, a truly ugly fortress in the middle of Mayfair. He was found in the consul's office, demanding to be given an explanation as to why he had been disqualified from going to Vietnam. On one occasion, Mr R came early to a session and locked himself in the toilet for a long while. This was not unusual, but when he lay down on the couch, he told me that he had tried to commit suicide in the toilet by drinking iodine from a bottle (which he had bought at the local chemist's on the way to the session). I was not sure whether to rush him to hospital straightaway. Though he was coughing and his voice sounded rather hoarse, he did not seem very sick. I decided to wait. Then he announced, 'I'm going to be reborn'. Soon afterwards, I found out exactly what he meant: he defecated in his pants while lying on the couch – an event which was going to be repeated a couple of times more during the treatment. In fact, Mr R had delusions of becoming a woman and giving birth to himself; he wanted to die so he could come back as a woman; he wished to create himself once again. For him, to go to Vietnam was to have the likely chance of dying, so he would be sent back home in a coffin covered by an American flag; he would be then reunited with mother in glory, she would love him for ever. Mr R was caught in a deluded maintenance of a prenatal union with mother, never to be torn apart.

Mr R (like Tony) wanted to paralyse time. He lived a mummified existence; his actions were frozen acts without a morrow (Minkowski 1933). The deliria of schizophrenic patients seemed to be permanently crystallised in their fragmentation, forever running in the same place. This is reflected in schizophrenic coprophagy, in which there is 'a rejection of the irreversible character of physiological processes . . . which conditions the irreversibility of biological temporality' (Gabel 1963). Mr R wanted to eat his excrement just as Tony did. I never knew for sure whether he had ever done so or not. In the act of eating his own excrement, the schizophrenic denies having expelled it, denies even having had anything to expel. It is a model of what can be lost, and the attempt to reincorporate the excrement is not only to recover it; it is the denial of the very possibility of losing it. Mr R also masturbated every day, compulsively; he claimed that he was able to suck his penis and swallow his own sperm. He commented once, 'There is no waste this way.'

At the beginning of his treatment, Tony had a strong wish to be dead, a wish described by Laing as the result of a primary guilt, originating in the feeling that one has no right to live. Tony 'played dead' for a long time; he believed that if nothing moved, if he were able to keep things immobile and frozen, he could survive forever. If he was 'dead', he could not die nor could he kill (Laing 1960). Indeed, at the start of the treatment I thought of Tony as being dead-in-life. The psychoanalytic task of giving meaning to the psychotic patient's utterances in the analytic encounter could be summarised thus: *Who would bring life to what, and for whom?*

I was afraid that Tony would actually kill himself, but I was reassured by the fact that he had never actually attempted suicide. I was more concerned he would choose to withdraw completely, become truly catatonic. He felt a genuine terror of living; he wanted to anticipate danger and control his fears by entering a kind of psychic hibernation; he would then be able to hold on to his objects forever, never experiencing any loss. Nevertheless, the term 'experiencing a loss' would not accurately describe Tony's feelings; it was rather a fear of disintegration, a destruction of his being, a real catastrophe. To this he opposed the omnipotent fantasy of paralysing time, eliminating the differences between being alive and being dead. He lived in a permanent state of ontological contradiction. He experienced himself as living at both extremes of an emotional spectrum, encompassing impotence as well as omnipotence. While at a given moment he felt at the centre of the universe, determining and controlling the movements of people and the shape of things to come, he also imagined himself at the capricious mercy of malevolent external agencies. Every emotion, every affect, every fantasy was always matched by its opposite. Solipsistic grandeur was accompanied by the loss of a sense of self. Euphoria, secretly created by a well-guarded feeling of being in control of the universe, was matched by the nausea caused by the imaginary destruction of the world. Nevertheless, the subject possesses an inner organisation that will help him to modify original failures. I witnessed in Tony 'the basic urge that patients have towards becoming normal' (Winnicott 1965). If transference is repetition (following thus the unconscious designs of the death instinct), it also creates the possibility for something new, something different, a new beginning. In the context of the analytic encounter, a very special, unique intimacy develops between patient and analyst. Whatever happens in the transference situation is unpredictable, and the same can be said of love. Love is not just a repetition of a pattern from the past. An analysis might allow for new (love-)objects to emerge but, as Loewald has clarified it for us, it is more relevant to think in terms of the analytic process facilitating a *new discovery* of objects, rather than a discovery of new objects (Loewald 1960: 225).

What helped Tony towards his recovery? A subject, in order to remain sane, or to be saved from psychosis, needs somebody, an other who can offer proof of 'a certain complicity and closeness with the subject's thoughts and theories' (Aulagnier 1975: 168). The French word, *complicité*, has been mistranslated. In French, as well as Spanish, it refers to a close understanding between people. The nature of this *complicité* is clear. It is a way of letting the psychotic patient know that one is on his side; there is a commitment on the part of the analyst which needs to be made explicit – even if not actually spoken; the wish to help cannot be denied, hidden, or fudged.

The analyst might be scared by the passionate involvement of the patient (a subject just like the analyst) who wants to be unconditionally loved. The analyst has to accept the risk. This does not, by itself, compromise the psychoanalytic attitude and the professional boundaries demanded and required from an analyst. When the madness of the patient's love borders on psychosis, it is not only scary for the analyst, but also exhausting. The analyst is forced to fight a war against the patient's destructiveness, his negative therapeutic reactions, the repeated splitting, the acting out. The intensity of the transference created by the 'diabolical device of the Viennese doctor' (Kristeva 1983: 9) can be extraordinary. Can we conceive of an analysis without transference, without the love generated by transference? Love is at the centre of transference, making all frustrations (including the sexual ones) bearable to the patient. It is *Liebe*, true libido, which helps the subject open up his self to another subject and form a relationship with him. The sexual, never separated from love, never forgotten even if repressed, will be there. The patient might ask to be loved by the analyst at all costs, at times asking for a mutual pact of negation of reality.

Frequently, masochism occupies central stage: 'Seduce me, please abuse me, do with me whatever you like, I want to prove my love to you,' demands the patient, translating his original need for survival into a traumatic need for love and recognition. It can be argued that there is a 'perverse' side to the analytic contract: one subject imposes on another subject certain conditions which, if accepted, enable the relationship to take place. The patient is supposed to tell every possible sexual fantasy, every dream, the details of intimate relationships to the analyst – who refuses to say much at all about himself. A power game? It can develop into one. The analyst's ethical commitment consists of not just *not* misusing this power, but refusing the position of power altogether in the first place. (This necessary refusal makes training analyses, at times, especially difficult.)

As in a caricature (where certain normal features of a person are exaggerated and yet remain recognisable), here one can see the risks of the analytic enterprise in the analysis of the psychotic. Tony did not want to accept reality, the separation between him and me, the differentiation of sexes or the generational conflict; he experienced total love for an all-omnipotent, idealised object. The 'as if' of the analytic encounter was lost and denied for most of the initial, psychotic period of treatment; instead, he harboured the impossible hope that I could be everything for him forever.

I would agree with Herbert Rosenfeld's contention as regards the careful need to assess the patient's vulnerability and defensiveness (Rosenfeld 1987). The idealisation of the analyst might be the only experience of love available to the patient; the analyst's attempts at interpreting the idealised transference could provoke a detrimental increase of the patient's envy and unnecessary experiences of humiliation. This demands from the analyst a prudent and watchful consideration of his countertransference; the patient's needs might be confused with the analyst's own neurotic desires. The narcissistic needs of the analyst can easily prolong the period of transference idealisation. And yet:

> It is important not to interfere with a patient's idealization of the analyst *just on principle*. A patient may have to make considerable progress in the analysis before he can accept the ups and downs of the analytic relationship, the battles which have to be fought, and the despair and emptiness which often seem unbearable.
>
> (Rosenfeld 1987: 271, italics added)

Although he was strongly criticised (and dismissed) by some of his Kleinian colleagues at the time of the publication of his book, I find Rosenfeld's clinical stance in this respect not only accurate but also courageous. It is, no doubt, a complex and difficult question whether and when to interpret or not interpret the idealised transference. This is, after all, a clinical decision, taken by the analyst after careful consideration of the patient's vulnerability as much as a thorough analysis of the analyst's own narcissistic needs. Nevertheless, this is easier said than done. The analyst's clinical judgement is constantly at risk of being misled by the dynamics of projections and introjections taking place in the analytic encounter.

I would not suggest that the analyst should *never* interpret the idealised transference – only that this can wait, can be postponed. One of the main tasks on the part of the analyst is to receive the patient's projective identifications (Money-Kyrle 1956); this necessarily implies the need to *accept* them and contain them.[5] There is plenty of time in an analysis to interpret those projections at the appropriate moment. In the analysis of Tony, I found that the idealised transference co-existed and perhaps even facilitated the intensely negative feelings sometimes expressed in the letters he wrote to me. One set of feelings did not exclude the other.

No subject can assume that he is capable of love. To be able to love is as uncertain as to know with certainty that one is lovable. Disturbed patients can experience an intense sense of shame and unbearable pain when they find (in the process of an analysis) that their capacity for love is greatly diminished. It can throw them into further desolation and hopelessness. Envy and destructiveness can be made worse by their desperate need for help. Their experience of vulnerability (feeling at the mercy of the analyst's designs) may increase the murderous attacks of their internal objects; this, in turn, makes the relationship with the analyst fraught with danger.

If patient and analyst have a therapeutic relationship over a long period of time, each of them becomes an inevitable witness to changes in the other. I cannot account for the way that Tony saw me (and my practice) change over the years. I am aware that he was particularly sensitive to all changes, including the variations of my mood, the way that I would phrase a question or my tone of voice when I made an interpretation. The importance of these things in the treatment of disturbed patients has often been noted. On the other hand, there has been a certain reluctance to admit, in the psychoanalytic literature and clinical presentations, how much liking or not liking the patient affects the therapeutic factors of an analysis. While it is not a necessary condition, liking a patient might play an important part in the treatment of patients. This is not to say that by itself it will help; nevertheless, it might, for example, affect the analyst's level of tolerance for the patient's regressive behaviour and destructiveness.

This presents a serious dilemma for the psychoanalyst treating patients originally identified by Rosenfeld as 'thick-skinned', characterised by their insensitivity to deeper feelings (Rosenfeld 1987). These are patients who are especially capable of provoking rejection in the analyst through their attempts at devaluing any form of help. In these cases, it might be difficult to discriminate between (a) a proper countertransference reaction (which can potentially be understood, contained and eventually 'given back' to the patient through interpretations); and (b) a genuine dislike that inhibits understanding. Ideally, we should be able to distinguish countertransference (a response to the patient's transference), from the analyst's *inevitable* transference to the patient. Given the often violent intensity of the analyst's countertransference reactions in the analysis of psychotic patients, liking or not liking a patient could be a decisive factor in their treatment. If this is accepted as an analytic parameter, the analyst is better able to deal with phenomena like hate in the countertransference. The analyst constantly moves from the maternal to the paternal position in the analysis of psychotic patients. He can never quite rest in one place, is always challenged to make urgent clinical decisions: either he offers a holding that makes the patient feel gratified and contained, or he establishes boundaries and differences (a handling) through the provisional meaning offered by his interpretations. In both cases, the analyst's aim is to promote the creation of a psychic space, even though this space is formed through the vicissitudes of an impossible and inevitably idealised love.

Freud declared that 'the cure is effected by love' (1906). The list of psychoanalytic authors who seemed to have misread, forgotten, misinterpreted or distorted what Freud actually said is too long to be quoted. Freud, in his letter to Jung, was referring to 'the fixation of the libido prevailing in the unconscious (transference)' (Letter to Jung, 6/12/1906); in other words, he was clearly talking here about the (transference-)love of the analysand, not about the libidinal effects of the analyst's presence or actions. The love of the analyst is *not* the curative force in the treatment. While the patient will be destined by the transference situation to love his analyst, the analyst loves the patient inasmuch as he is able to put himself in the patient's place, to identify needs and wishes in the patient. The analyst is perhaps strangely but rightly detached from his love for the patient, from his identification. This is another analytic paradox: the love of the analyst is only possible because of his detachment (see Kristeva 1983). This detached love will allow him to manage the patient's persecutory anxieties and reactions of hate, a task more relevant to making a psychoanalysis successful than the naive belief that 'love' is the curative force (Friedman 1998: 171). In spite of what some of the authors of the inter-subjective school suggest, the relationship between patient and analyst is never the same for both subjects. The intensity of the patient's transference only occurs because of the lack of symmetry in the relationship; this creates a tension in the analytic relationship between asymmetry and mutuality, a tension that needs to be kept, not dissolved

(Modell 1990; Hoffer 1996). Lacan called it 'subjective disparity' (1960–61).

As generous as the analyst's love may be on occasion, detachment allows the analyst truly to understand the absurdity of the desire contained in the passionate declarations spoken by his patient. Winnicott spoke of the importance of the 'distance between analyst and patient' (1960: 161). If this distance did not exist, then the analyst might take the patient's declarations of love as the irrefutable proof of his personal qualities and attractiveness. The love of the analyst for the patient is combined, but not confused, with love for the task, for the work; these facets cannot effectively work without each other. To be an analyst requires a degree of fervour, of passion for the ideas that the theory of psychoanalysis offers. More than anything else, it is this passion which keeps him alive, real, and good enough for his patients. Also, the analyst will feel genuinely close to his patient whenever the latter allows the former to *analyse him*; that is, when the insight offered by the analyst is accepted, taken in, and used by the patient for his own benefit – not just to please the analyst. These moments are particularly important when they have been preceded by a period of negativity and malignant resistance in the work of the analysis (Priscilla Roth 2003, private communication).

Complicité and closeness were manifested in my relationship with Tony through the use of humour. Even though he suffered the horror of being paralysed in an emotional trap where life was inconceivable and death the only alternative, Tony saved himself by having a strong sense of humour; although black and surrealistic, it contained the expression of hope. Humour at some stages of the treatment constituted 'the currency of intimacy' (Cohen 1999) between us; in a true dialectical way, humour actually *created* and *established* this intimacy, которая I suspect made Tony trust that he did not need to explain everything to me, nor did I have to spell out every interpretation to him. To quote Cohen's book on jokes:

> When we laugh at the same thing, that is a very special occasion. It is already noteworthy that we laugh at all, at anything, and that we laugh all alone. That we do it *together* is the satisfaction of a deep human longing, the realization of a desperate

hope. It is the hope that we are enough like one another to sense one another, to be able to live together.

(Cohen 1999: 29)

Access to his humour depended on Tony's moods, which were subject to great variation. Through his capacity for humour, Tony created a self-contained psychic environment where the madness of his mother could be kept at bay, excluded, in an area outside the self. If, at certain times, he would make fun of his mother's madness, humour served the essential purpose of enabling Tony to laugh at himself. There was also an implicit acknowledgement, present in both of us, that this was a precarious enterprise: there was no guarantee that the other would actually laugh at a given humorous intervention. Jokes and laughter could emerge at the most painful times, and I was wary of 'celebrating' what could have been manic reactions on Tony's part. Humour was also part of a literary sensitivity that made Tony appreciate the writings of Lautréamont, André Breton, Dylan Thomas, Rimbaud, Allen Ginsberg and Baudelaire, as well as punk rock, the Ramones, Buñuel, and Latin American writers like José Donoso and Gabriel García Márquez. While punk rock and the Ramones' music and lyrics on madness never appealed to me, Tony's literary and cinematic preferences did bring us closer.

I was grateful – and lucky – that Tony found his way to my consulting room. For his part, Tony was also grateful: he too considered himself to have been lucky and referred several times to the element of chance that had brought us together. Chance enough to determine our fate, as Freud would have it (1910: 137).

At an early stage in his analysis, Tony had reminded himself of a Rolling Stones' song: if one could not always get what one wanted, one should at least try; perhaps, sometimes, one might just get what one needs. Towards the end of his analysis, he thought he had got some of the things he needed to make life worth living. He further developed a small business he had started, bought himself a house, had a girlfriend, and lived an independent life. Nevertheless, there was no happy ending; we both knew and acknowledged that these were not things that proved his sanity, nor were they the result of a complete cure. He was prone to serious periods of depression, but these did not prevent him from enjoying himself and his freedom. It was to Tony's credit that he was able to accept the irony of the psychoanalytic situation: he created me as the object that he needed, but then he had to reconcile himself with the fact that I was not it. He renounced the omnipotence of his wishes. Love, in the time of madness, managed to keep one up on psychosis. When the analysis came to an end, we both knew that it could have gone on forever.

'BETWEEN THE FEAR OF MADNESS AND THE NEED TO BE MAD'

Psychoanalysts tend to present their successful cases to the public, rather than their failures. Nevertheless, we still know relatively little about what really makes an analysis a success. Ironically, in spite of the abundance of psychoanalytic writings, it is easier to reflect on what makes it a failure.

Joan Riviere tells us that one day during her analysis, Freud made an interpretation to which she responded with an objection: 'He then said: "It is *unconscious*." I was overwhelmed then,' she confessed, 'by the realization that I knew nothing about it' (Riviere 1958). Any true psychoanalytic insight carries with it this feeling of being overwhelmed, not so much by the discovery of something new as by the fact that we did not know about it. Far from being a mere intellectual exercise, or at the opposite end a purely cathartic one, psychoanalysis demands from the patient, first, a certain *capacity for humility*, which enables the subject to stand knowing so little about himself. This is independent of the presenting complaints, the degree of pathological disturbance, or the social circumstances. In the second place, psychoanalysis demands the existence of a *conflict of suffering*. As far as I know, Freud only used the concept of *Leidenskonflikt* once, in a letter to Edoardo Weiss: he believed that only a conflict that provoked suffering can motivate the subject to look for a cure. Then Freud proceeded to make the unusual suggestion that one should get rid of those patients that do not suffer. One should 'ship them overseas, let us say to South America, and let them look for and find their destiny there' (Freud and Weiss 1920).

Tony proved he could fulfil these two requirements: he was capable of humility, and he felt enough motivation through his suffering to search for and accept therapeutic help. There is still a third important condition also required by psychoanalysis that Tony fulfilled: what Freud described as the possession of a 'fairly reliable character' (1905: 263). As Guy Thompson has remarked: 'the need for a reliable character can't be emphasised too highly'. He rightly argues that this is a 'prerequisite of treatment, not its consequence' (Thompson 1994). In other words, a poor character cannot be treated. Chronic liars and pathological deceivers, for example, cannot overcome their lies and their deceptions. Nina Coltart was one clinician who gave explicit importance to 'moral character' or 'ethical reliability' in the clinical assessment of patients for psychoanalysis (Coltart 1987). Once, in referring to me a patient whom I argued was too disturbed for analysis, Coltart insisted: 'Maybe, but he is *decent*.'

In *The Question of Lay Analysis* (1926), Freud described fairly common human situations as part of the motivation for people to seek psychoanalytic treatment: fluctuations in moods, a sense of despondency and insecurity, 'nervous embarrassment among strangers', 'difficulties in carrying out his professional work', 'feelings of anxiety', inhibition from walking on the streets alone or travelling by train, headaches, fainting spells, difficulties in their sexuality. People went to doctors, who offered them ineffectual forms of treatment which gave them temporarily relief, or none at all. When eventually the disappointed patients arrived at the analyst's consulting room, they were faced with the fact that 'Nothing takes place between (patient and analyst) except that *they talk to each other*' (p. 187, italics added). A patient, Freud continued, had to accept the existence of 'things in himself that he would be very unwilling to tell other people [. . .] and other things that one would not care to admit to *oneself*'. This already represented a 'great advance in psychological self-knowledge', but then something else happens, 'a very remarkable psychological problem begins to appear'. In the situation of treatment, the patient becomes aware 'of a thought of his own being kept secret from his own self. It looks as though his own self were no longer the unity which he had always considered it to be, as though there were something else as well in him that could confront that self' (p. 188).

It is this notion – that there is no unity within one's self – which constitutes for some the most revolutionary aspect of Freud's ideas (Rorty 1989, 1991). When the subject is capable of accepting the existence of a psychic reality alien to himself, when he recognises that his self contains something secret, or different, or contradictory to his wishes and thoughts, and that this *something* might be part of a conflict which is making him suffer, we say that he is psychologically minded (Coltart 1987, 1988). The subject can contemplate the idea that anything that takes place in that psychic scenario – even the most inexplicable psychological event – might have meaning, and thus is worth thinking about. Absurd dreams, the strangest of symptoms, contradictory memories that seem to come from nowhere, or bizarre thoughts arising from events of everyday life, they are all the result of a dynamic process which originates in an area of darkness, the consequence of unconscious conflicts *unknown* to us. The analyst is not there to teach the meaning of his actions to the patient; he is not there to cure him, indoctrinate him or save him. Instead, through listening, he tries not to interfere with the mutual process of learning from the other. The patient's speech becomes meaningful through the analyst's listening, which changes the narrative offered by the patient. It is never the same to tell a dream to a friend or a spouse than to tell it to one's analyst but it is not the analyst who creates the meaning of the dream for the patient. The unconscious meaning unfolds exclusively through the discourse of the patient, revealed, as it were, by the analyst's capacity to listen.

Once Tony had found his way to my consulting room, he proved to be psychologically minded. He offered me the opportunity to treat somebody who, while being seriously disturbed and for a long while psychotic, was able to respond to psychoanalytic treatment. Tony considered mental hospitals and the people working in them as part of a much hated *establishment* which included other figures of authority: the police, doctors, priests, the government, judges and lawyers. This antagonism was one of the manifest reasons for refusing psychiatric treatment, and to seek psychotherapy instead. He was helped by a mother, who, while very disturbed, was histrionic enough to wish to be seen by her children as 'cool' and enlightened. After the death of his father, Tony had felt that his life had ended: he withdrew into himself, became a failure at school and could not see any future for himself; he was going to become a bum, a cripple, a dropout. Nevertheless, he was not yet psychotic. Only after taking drugs was he pushed over the edge towards a mental breakdown. At that point, he could have possibly ended up as a patient in a psychiatric institution. I have known several cases of people with a similar initial psychotic presentation who became (perhaps unnecessarily) more or less chronic psychiatric patients. Some of these cases were seriously disturbed, with a florid psychotic presentation at the beginning of the treatment; others suffered from consecutive acute episodes.

When Tony started therapy with me, I was involved with what was known as the anti-psychiatry movement in the UK. I was privileged to have lived for a time in a small therapeutic community with psychotic people in Archway, North London. My previous training as a clinical psychologist in Argentina in the late 1960s had been profoundly influenced by psychoanalysis. Although non-medical people were not allowed to train then at the only Argentinian psychoanalytic institute of the time, psychologists were taught at the university, and privately encouraged, supervised, and analysed by members of the local psychoanalytic society (who were, at the time, mainly Kleinian). Through the influence of the writings of Bion, Hanna Segal and Herbert Rosenfeld, the visits of British analysts, the teachings of people like Enrique Pichon-Rivière and José Bleger, it was not unusual for clinicians to treat disturbed patients in their private psychoanalytic practices. Pichon-Rivière had published his 'Psicoanálisis de la Esquizofrenia' in 1947, the same year that Rosenfeld published his first paper on the 'Analysis of a Schizophrenic State with Depersonalisation' (1947). This was only one year after Melanie Klein's 'Notes on Some Schizoid Mechanisms'. Pichon-Rivière had also been one of the official presenters at the *XIV Congrès des Psychoanalystes de Langue Francaise*, where he read his paper 'Quelques observations sur le transfert chez des patients psychotiques' (1952). In similar fashion to his Kleinian colleagues from Europe, Pichon-Rivière thought that schizophrenic patients were capable of intense transferences (in spite of their extreme defensive withdrawal from reality). He believed that their treatment should be centred on the analysis of the transference and the mechanism of projective identification.

At the beginning of my practice in London in 1970, I treated along psychoanalytic lines a number of patients in private practice who had been (or would have been) diagnosed as schizophrenic. At the time, this was not necessarily the prevailing culture of the antipsychiatry groups with which I was involved. R. D. Laing (who had been trained as a psychoanalyst in the British Society) and his colleagues were critical not only of psychiatrists, but also of the 'orthodoxy' of psychoanalysts. Nevertheless, I had come from a psychoanalytic tradition that taught me that psychoanalysis, unlike psychiatry, was not concerned with restraining or subduing madness. Therefore, there was no contradiction, in principle, between questioning of psychiatry on the one hand and the clinical practice of psychoanalysis on the other.

Perhaps today, more than 40 years after *The Divided Self* was first published, it is difficult to understand how innovative was the shift suggested by Laing's work for many contemporary clinicians in the UK. He considered the experience of the psychotic as a *true* experience, rather than as a falsified one. He did not insist on doubting the immediate subjective experience of the psychotic; this never meant that the patient was not psychotic, or that his psychosis should not be treated. Laing restored a sense of respect for all psychotic phenomena as something strange, alien, perhaps beyond interpretation. Like Freud many years earlier, he challenged clinicians to listen to patients, even those who appeared hopelessly mad. The psychotic (in all of us) refers to something unknowable, elusive to any kind of certainty. At times, the analyst treating psychotic patients might glimpse this through an act of intuition, a gut reaction which makes him 'burst out' with an inexplicable clinical intervention. Then, the analyst gets closer (in himself as much as in his patient) to something that otherwise remains unspoken, out of reach. Since psychosis might elude definition, Laing argued, it might not be accessible to any form of simplified psychological resolution. Insanity is not *just* unreason, nor is it necessarily a failure of reason. Even if the psychotic does not know what to do with his knowledge, he may often have a disconcerting, accurate insight into his madness. This accounts for the psychotic patients' rather inspired insights, a self-conscious awareness which nevertheless produces so much suffering and deception of self and others. Traditionally, if the clinical presentation of a patient included hallucinations and delusions, a loss of capacity to relate to others, and if he appeared to be detached, unresponsive, and negativistic, a diagnosis of schizophrenia was likely to be made. Even today, the diagnosis of schizophrenia seems to depend, at least partly, on the ideology and conception of illness held by the clinician. Nevertheless, the symptoms mentioned above might indeed be indicative of such a condition, but not necessarily so. It is an unavoidable tragedy that sometimes such diagnoses can only be confirmed with the passing of time, when the progression of the illness brings about a deterioration of the subject's capacity for relatedness. Even this seems to be put in question by those cases of schizophrenia that present themselves as a series of acute episodes without the above-mentioned deterioration. It might be worth mentioning here, in this respect, a related diagnosis, that of *bouffées delirantes*, which is a concept that has been exclusively developed and used in France. It was traditionally closely associated to severe forms of hysteria and describes acute episodes characterised by the sudden eruption of a transitory psychosis which can last from a few weeks to a few months. The most important diagnostic aspect of the breakdown is its sudden character. Otherwise, it presents very similar features to a proper schizophrenic breakdown: numerous and exuberant hallucinations, paranoid ideas, sexual confusion, delusions of grandeur, etc. I often thought that Tony could have been diagnosed as suffering from this type of hallucinatory acute psychosis, which can sometimes be precipitated by the use of drugs (Ey *et al.* 1965).

It can be argued that a considerable number of the seriously ill patients found in the literature and seen in our consulting rooms might be disturbed hysterics after all. Perhaps, the diagnosis of *hysterical psychosis* could be rescued (Maleval 1981; Libbrecht 1995). This certainly would make sense to most psychiatrists but not necessarily to psychoanalysts. Plenty of patients would fit this clinical description; there are hysterical patients who are undoubtedly psychotic. Nevertheless, the structural reasons or theoretical justification to place hysteria among the psychoses would be highly questionable.

Bion established the important difference between psychotic and non-psychotic personalities co-existing within one subject. According to him, the difference between the two personalities depends on the splitting of everything that concerns awareness of internal and external reality, and the expulsion into, or the engulfing of objects (Bion 1957). The preponderance of destructive impulses, being so intense in disturbed patients, turns their love impulses into sadism. There is a hatred of reality (a point originally made by Freud 1924b: 149), together with a dread of imminent annihilation. Bion also suggested that there is '... a premature and precipitate formation of object relations, foremost amongst which is the transference, whose thinness is in marked contrasts with the tenacity with which they are maintained. The prematurity, thinness and tenacity are pathognomonic' (p. 44). This seems to have been confirmed by many other clinicians. A patient who suffers from separation anxiety at the first weekend of the analysis − as if he had been coming for treatment for years − would lead me indeed to consider this reaction pathognomonic of serious borderline pathology.

In the case of Tony, his psychotic personality seemed to co-exist with his non-psychotic one in a way that allowed his ego not to be wholly withdrawn from reality. The non-psychotic personality was never obscured by the psychotic one. While the prematurity and the tenacity were certainly present in Tony's transference from the beginning, the thinness was not. His analysis was conducted for a long period of time under the dominance of an idealised transference, which remained mostly untouched. While this helped him to avoid further feelings of vulnerability (Rosenfeld 1987), it also allowed him to express his true despair, his sense of being lost in the world, and his wish to be helped. This should not be seen as a technical suggestion equivalent to active encouragement through reassurance or expressions of love (as suggested by Waelder; Federn; and Jacobson), nor as an attempt to provide a new and better parent in the figure of the analyst, who would compensate for the environmental failures of the past (Fromm-Reichmann 1950).

There will always be an intense pressure exerted on the analyst by disturbed and perverse patients (this is not, of course, an exclusive list) to give up the psychoanalytic setting. I always found it most useful and certainly safest, for the patient and for the analyst, to adhere to a psychoanalytic mode of working. This mode cannot and should not be rigid. Herbert Rosenfeld, Donald Winnicott and Hanna Segal, three of the four leading British analysts (the other being Wilfred Bion), who promoted the treatment of psychotic patients using the 'essentials' of the psychoanalytic technique, introduced changes in their analytic approach. Although Rosenfeld and Segal described these changes as 'minor changes' and 'minor deviations' (Rosenfeld 1987: 311; Segal 1950: 101), they can be seen – at least in the case of Winnicott and Rosenfeld, both of whom gave more details of their technique – as fairly substantial. For example, Rosenfeld did not ask schizophrenic patients to lie down on the couch, many of them were 'better treated in the sitting-up position' (p. 65); he saw them *at least* six times a week; he did not take long breaks (not more than a few days) while treating patients in an acute state of psychosis; and more importantly, gave the patients 'if necessary, longer sessions (ninety minutes) while the acute phase persists' (p. 66).

Given the confusion between thought and action on the part of disturbed patients, these measures might seem 'minor' to the analyst but they may not be so for the patient, who interprets them as non-verbal forms of reassurance and expressions of love. Winnicott says: 'For the neurotic, the couch and warmth and comfort can be *symbolical* of the mother's love; for the psychotic it would be more true to say that these things *are* the analyst's expression of love. The couch *is* the analyst's lap or womb, and the warmth *is* the live warmth of the analyst's body. And so on' (1947). This certainly proved to have been the case with Tony. I decided, after the second year of analysis, to change from the 90-minute sessions that I had been offering him up to then (following the example of Rosenfeld and other colleagues, like Enid Balint, personal communication) to the usual 50 minutes. I became aware that *I did not want* to offer him prolonged sessions any longer; I did not wish to treat him in any 'special' way. Not surprisingly, Tony reacted with anger, resentment and actual physical tantrums during the sessions. He refused to leave the room, claiming that he was not going to allow me to love other patients more than I loved him. It took time, hard work and a lot of trust on his part for Tony to accept that it was not a matter of loving others more than him, but that – considering the fact that he might have been the only patient I was seeing for prolonged sessions – I was choosing *not* to love him more than others.

The relevance of keeping a proper psychoanalytic setting becomes very important here. The regularity of the sessions, the reliability of the analyst, the attention given to the patient, the adherence to an interpretative mode, the working through of psychic conflicts, all this offers the possibility for psychotic patients to find a slow, painful recovery. It is the consistency of the psychoanalytic setting that allows for what Winnicott called 'moments of illusion' to occur:

> At the start, simple *contact* with external or shared reality has to be made, by the infant's hallucinating and the world's presenting, with moments of illusion for the infant in which the two are taken by him to be identical, which they never in fact are.
> (Winnicott 1945: 154)

At times, Tony had difficulties in believing that I existed; he was obviously relieved to see me at the following session. I thought that Tony hallucinated my existence; he created me through his desires. This could be something that disturbed patients *need* to do. To interpret it as a negative, regressive action would only interfere with the process of recovery. To encourage it through unnecessary so-called supportive interventions on the part of the analyst could be seductive and/or detrimental.

When Winnicott spoke of 'moments of illusion' he was referring to the beginning of life, the moment of the encounter of mother and baby. By now, most of us have heard it many times: if it is true that there is no such thing as an infant without a mother, then it is also equally true that there is no such thing as a mother and baby without a father, imaginary or real. The analytic encounter itself cannot be understood in terms of *just* the mother and baby relationship. Mother and baby can only exist in the context of a third term, which does not need to be physically present in order to be *there*.

The third term (albeit not the only one) of all analyses, which regulates the relationship between patient and analyst, is defined and made present by the *psychoanalytic setting*. This notion was elaborated in the 1960s by Enrique Pichon-Rivière in his teachings. The importance of maintaining a proper setting (including whatever modifications the analyst might decide to introduce) can be better understood through the analysis that Bleger (a disciple of Pichon-Rivière) made of the psychoanalytic frame. He defined the *frame* as a permanent presence, a stable non-process. While the process is always variable (it constitutes the material of the sessions and can be studied, analysed and interpreted), the frame forms the background of a unique Gestalt. The frame is a 'dumb' institution defined by the psychoanalytic contract, which establishes the formal terms of the arrangements agreed by patient and analyst. It is always there, possibly used at times as a defence against psychotic anxiety, similar to the way that we tend to use institutions (Jacques 1955), or as a *depositary*[6] of the psychotic part of the personality (Bleger 1967). Bleger described it as the 'most primitive and undifferentiated organisation', never noticed unless it is missing, which receives the projection of the patient's 'ghost world'. The psychoanalytic frame helps patient and analyst to know that whatever else is going on in the analysis, the analysis *continues*. The frame exists in the mind of the analyst and it is up to him to preserve it, trust in it, to have the ability to use it. The existence and preservation of this frame, and the analyst's own basic trust in the psychoanalytic process, are the conditions for the moments of illusion to be created. The analytic frame also serves the function of protecting the patient over the course of the analysis, in comparable fashion to the mother's role as a protective shield during the child's development (Khan 1963). If during a long analysis there were breaches and failures of the frame, these can produce a cumulative trauma, which develops in silent and invisible ways, achieving nevertheless the value of trauma, if only in retrospect. Many instances of analytic impasse (as described by Rosenfeld 1987) could be the result, as much as the proof, of the presence of this cumulative process.

Tony seemed to have used the frame as a very effective depositary of the psychotic part of his personality. At the beginning of his treatment, Tony's fate appeared to be sealed; he was paralysed in time and seemed to be destined to remain forever self-institutionalised. A certain degree of self-institutionalisation is part of any normal development. In growing up, the human subject is by necessity forced to unconsciously surrender to the other's desire. It is a process of social learning by which the individual's subjectivity *becomes*. The social environment imposes this learning on the subject, who gives up or tones down his unconscious desires for the price of survival, acceptance and recognition (Castoriadis 1997; see also Balibar 1994; Fryer 2004). A process of desubjectivation allows subjectivity to develop. However, it is never to be fully achieved or completed, otherwise one would witness the triumph of the death instinct at the service of the Other. (At a socio-political level, tyrannical, totalitarian and repressive governments attempt and at times unfortunately succeed in imposing extreme forms of desubjectivation on their citizens. In western democratic countries there is growing concern about the restrictions and controls imposed by their political leaders and government figures, such measures being justified through rationalised versions of an overprotective and religious morality.)

The subject has to remain free to recreate meaning, to be unpredictable, to surprise himself and others through his actions. The alternative is to inhabit a self that functions similarly to a protective institution; like a jail or a hospital, a family or a neighbourhood, the institutionalised self becomes a safe refuge which the fading subject would be unwilling to leave. There are two basic fears, which determine this process. One is the fear of change; the other is the fear of attack (Pichon-Rivière 1967). These fears make the subject reluctant to move away from an emotional status quo already achieved, refusing to face any new situation. This process can progressively become a tragic and pathological cul-de-sac, a passive adaptation to a reality that is experienced as menacing and hostile (Kohon 1999). A depressive apathy as regards any possibility of change might ensue. There is a lack of initiative, together with a loss of interest in the outside world; these subjects appear submissive to others but the only safe place they can find is their very illness. They develop a way of being in the world which, through sterile repetition, falsely promises a personal safety net.

Through a destructive element embedded in their persistence in being, their illness may remain relatively contained within their rigid measures of psychical safety. We might only learn about their madness through their acting out in the process of treatment (hence the value of such acting out in psychoanalysis). On the other hand (in obsessional patients, for example) the madness will be expressed only in their compulsive thoughts; this confinement might help to keep themselves sane; the madness is limited to an area, keeping the rest of their personality fairly safe.

In the process of becoming a subject, we are inevitably at the mercy of external events over which we have no control. Nevertheless, we have to make our choices, to decide our destiny. While fate is irrevocable, destiny can be chosen. This is one reason why Freud spoke of a 'choice of neurosis', a concept that – however mysterious – confronts the problem of *why* and *how* a person may fall ill (1915: 317). In employing this concept, Freud implied that the subject *actively though unconsciously* participates in the illness. Only then, once the historical and constitutional determinants of an illness are assumed by the subject as a choice, do they become meaningful and 'attain the force of motivating factors' (Laplanche and Pontalis 1967). The same is implied in the Freudian concept of *object-choice*, a choice far removed from being a mere intellectual act. The subject's actions are determined by his unconscious, but that does not make him less responsible for them. 'Tragedy means, above all else,' says Alford (1992), 'that people are responsible without being free' (p. 115). Oedipus's fate was overdetermined (thus, not free) but he took symbolic responsibility for his actions when he declared that, although many of his sufferings were the work of Apollo, it was his own choice (carried out by his own hand) to blind himself. Freud's view in this regards is best illustrated by his appealing to an actual Austrian law when, in response to the Rat Man's objections to his interpretations, he said:

> . . . it is well known, of course, that it was equally punishable to say, 'The Emperor is an ass' or to disguise the forbidden words by saying 'If anyone says, etc., . . . then he will have me reckon with.
>
> (Freud: 1909d: 179)

Tony had enough courage to break away from his self-institutionalisation, finding for his destiny in diverse ways. For example, he refused electroshock treatment at the psychiatric hospital; he asked to be treated by psychotherapy; writing letters or bringing his dreams for analysis were active efforts on his part to gain control over his destiny. He declared that his mother and sister could have their madness back; that he was not going to Hell; that his mother could go by herself. In separating himself from his mother, Tony turned what could have been a pathetic fate into a dramatic destiny.

Winnicott, for all his clinical misjudgements and mistakes, seemed to have understood that madness is the most personal characteristic of a human being. If the subject is to feel alive, if he is to experience passion and be creative, then it might be necessary for him to accept that he will be 'forever caught in a conflict, nicely balanced between the fear of madness and the need to be mad' (Winnicott *et al.* 1989).

Paradox is the nature of the beast, the very subject of psychoanalytic inquiry. Madness (as much as love and art) remains somewhat beyond the reach of our understanding.

Notes

1 Rosenfeld mentioned this form in passing but he did not elaborate on it (1987).
2 The letters have been reproduced in their original spelling.
3 There may be good theoretical reasons to speak in terms of 'subject' rather than 'object' relationships (Kennedy 1998). This, of course, will not make psychoanalysis more or less 'inter-subjective' or 'humane'.
4 For an interesting elaboration of Laplanche's concepts, see Scarfone (2002).
5 Money-Kyrle's article on 'normal countertransference' seems at times theoretically too simple, and somehow clinically outdated. Nevertheless, it remains a 'classic', an inspiring source of further speculation and critical thought. Money-Kyrle talked in terms of both the analyst's reparative drives and the parental drives, as complements to Freud's concept of 'benevolent neutrality'. Recently, Britton has proposed the notion of an 'ordinary positive countertransference' (2003); he believes that one could take this for granted, as a 'natural' phenomenon, 'like the love of parents for children' (p. 55). Both of these authors, Money-Kyrle and Britton, seem to take, in this respect, the relationship between children and parents as too literal a model for the psychoanalytic situation.
6 In the translation of Bleger's paper, published in the *International Journal of Psycho-Analysis*, the term 'depository' was used. I prefer to use 'depositary'. The English 'depository' refers to a place, a thing or a receptacle where

something is deposited for safekeeping. In this sense, it is equivalent to 'repository', which is the word most commonly used in the psychoanalytic literature. In contrast, 'depositary' designates a persona, more than a thing, with whom anything material or immaterial is lodged in trust. It is closer to the original Spanish *depositario*, which conveys more acutely the vitality of the frame.

References

Alford, C. F. (1992) *The Psychoanalytic Theory of Greek Tragedy*, New Haven, CT/London: Yale University Press.
Aulagnier, P. (1975) *The Violence of Interpretation. From Pictogram to Statement*, London: Brunner-Routledge, 2001.
Balibar, E. (1994) 'Subjection and subjectivation', in J. Copjec (ed.) *Supposing the Subject*, New York: Verso.
Bion, W. R. (1957) 'Differentiation of the psychotic from the non-psychotic personalities', in *Second Thoughts*, London: Heinemann, 1967.
—— (1959) 'Attacks on linking', in *Second Thoughts*, London: Heinemann, 1967.
—— (1962) 'A theory of thinking', in *Second Thoughts*, London: Heinemann, 1967.
Bleger, J. (1967) 'Psycho-analysis of the psycho-analytic frame', *International Journal of Psycho-Analysis* 48: 511–519.
Britton, R. (2003) 'Hysteria (III): the erotic countertransference', in *Sex, Death and the Superego – Experiences in Psychoanalysis*, London: Karnac.
Bruner, J. (1990) *Acts of Meaning,* Cambridge, MA: Harvard University Press.
Byatt, A. S (1985) *Still Life*, New York: Macmillan.
Castoriadis, C. (1997) 'Psychoanalysis and politics', in *World in Fragments: Writings on Politics, Society, Psychoanalysis, and the Imagination*, Stanford: Stanford University Press.
Cohen, T. (1999) *Jokes – Philosophical Thought on Joking Matters*, Chicago: University of Chicago Press.
Coltart, N. (1987) 'Diagnosis and assessment for suitability for psychoanalytic psychotherapy', *British Journal of Psychotherapy* 4, 2; also included in *Slouching Towards Bethlehem . . . And Further Psychoanalytic Explorations*, London: Free Association Books, 1992.
—— (1988) 'The assessment of psychological-mindedness in the diagnostic interview', *British Journal of Psychiatry* 153: 819–820.
Eigen, M. (1999) *Toxic Nourishment,* London: Karnac.
Ey, H., Bernard, P. and Brisset, Ch. (1965) *Manuel de Psychiatrie*, Paris: Masson.
Freud, S. (1905) 'On psychotherapy', *S.E.* 7.
—— (1906) Letter to Jung (8F). In *The Freud/Jung Letters – The Correspondence between Sigmund Freud and C. G. Jung,* W. McGuire (ed.), Cambridge, MA: Harvard University Press, 1974 (1988).
Freud, S. (1909d) 'Notes upon a case of obsessional neurosis', *S.E.* 10.
—— (1910) *Leonardo Da Vinci and a Memory of his Childhood, S.E.* 11.

—— (1915) 'Observations on transference-love', S.E. 12.
—— (1920) Beyond the Pleasure Principle, S.E. 18.
—— (1923) The Ego and the Id, S.E. 19.
—— (1924b) 'Neurosis and psychosis', S.E. 19.
—— (1926) Inhibitions, Symptoms and Anxiety, S.E. 20.
—— (1926) The Question of Lay Analysis – Conversations with an Impartial Person, S.E. 20.
Freud, S. and Weiss, E. (1920) Problemas de la Práctica Psicoanalítica – Correspondencia Freud-Weiss. Barcelona: Gedisa, 1979.
Friedman, J. A. (1998) The Origins of Self and Identity – Living and Dying in Freud's Psychoanalysis, Northvale, NJ: Jason Aronson.
Fromm-Reichmann, F. (1950) Principles of Intensive Psychotherapy, Chicago: University of Chicago Press.
Fryer, D. R. (2004) The Intervention of the Other – Ethical Subjectivity in Levinas, and Lacan, New York: Other Press.
Gabel, J. (1963) La Fausse Conscience – Essai sur la Reification, Paris: Editions de Minuit.
Green, A. (1980) 'Passions and their vicissitudes. On the relation between madness and psychosis', in On Private Madness, London: Hogarth Press, 1986.
—— (2002) Time in Psychoanalysis – Some Contradictory Aspects, London: Free Association Books.
Hoffer, A. (1996) 'Asymmetry and mutuality in the analytic relationship: contemporary lessons from the Freud–Ferenczi dialogue', in A. Ferenczi Turn in Psychoanalysis, P.L. Rudnytsky, A. Bókay, and P. Giampieri-Deutsch (eds), New York: New York University Press.
Jacques, E. (1955) 'Social systems as a defence against persecutory and depressive anxiety', in M. Klein, P. Heimann and R. E. Money-Kyrle (eds) New Directions in Psycho-Analysis, London: Tavistock Publications, 1971.
Kennedy, R. (1998) The Elusive Human Subject – A Psychoanalytic Theory of Subject Relations, London: Free Association Books.
Khan, M. Masud R. (1963) 'The concept of cumulative trauma', in The Privacy of the Self, London: Hogarth Press, 1974.
Klein, M. (1946) 'Notes on some schizoid mechanisms', in The Writings of Melanie Klein, Vol. 3, London: Hogarth Press.
—— (1957) Envy and Gratitude. The Writings of Melanie Klein, Vol. 3, London: Hogarth Press.
Kohon, G. (1976) 'Nascita e morte nella schizophrenia', in A. Verdiglione (ed.) Il Diavolo sul Lettino – Psicosi e Follia, Venezia: Marsilio, 1977.
—— (1999) No Lost Certainties to be Recovered, London: Karnac.
Kristeva, J. (1983) Tales of Love, New York: Columbia, 1987.
Lacan, J. (1936 [1949]) 'The mirror stage as formative of the function of the I', in Ecrits: A Selection, London: Tavistock Publications, 1977.
—— (1960–61). Le Séminaire. Livre VIII. Le Tranfert, 1960–61, J.-A. Miller (ed.), Paris: Seuil, 1991.

Laing. R. D. (1960) *The Divided Self. An Existential Study in Sanity and Madness*, London: Tavistock Publications.
Laplanche, J. (1956) 'Implantation, intromission', in J. Laplanche *Essays on Otherness*, London and New York: Routledge, 1999.
—— (1987) *New Foundations for Psychoanalysis*, Oxford: Blackwell.
Laplanche, J. and Pontalis, J.-B. (1967) *The Language of Psycho-Analysis*, London: Hogarth Press.
Libbrecht, K. (1995) *Hysterical Psychosis – A Historical Survey*, New Brunswick and London: Transaction Publishers.
Loewald, H. (1960) 'On the therapeutic action of psychoanalysis', *International Journal of Psycho-Analysis* 41:16–33.
Maleval. J.-C. (1981) *Folies Hystériques e Psychoses Dissociatives*, Paris: Payot.
Minkowski, E. (1933) *Lived Time: Phenomenological and Psychopathological Studies*, Evanston: Northwestern University Press, 1970.
Modell, A. (1990) *Other Times, Other Realities*, Cambridge, MA: Harvard University Press.
Money-Kyrle, R. (1956) 'Normal counter-transference and some of its deviations', *International Journal of Psycho-Analysis* 37: 360–366; also included in *The Collected Papers of Roger Money-Kyrle*, Clunie Press, 1978.
Muller, J. P. (1996) 'Beyond the psychoanalytic dyad – developmental semiotics', in *Freud, Pierce, and Lacan*, New York: Routledge.
Pichon-Rivière, E. J. (1947) 'Psicoanálisis de la esquizofrenia', *Revista Psiconanalítica* 4: 614–618.
—— (1952) 'Quelques observations sur le transfert chez des patients psychotiques', *Revue Française Psychoanalitique*, 16: 254–258; also published as 'Algunas observaciones sobre la transferencia en pacientes psicóticos', *Revista de Psicoanálisis* 18: 2, 1961.
—— (1965) *Lecciones de Psicología Social*, Buenos Aires: Primera Escuela Privada de Psiquiatría.
—— (1967) 'Introducción a una nueva problemática de la psiquiatría', *Acta psiquiátrica y Psicologica América Latina* 13, 4: 355–365.
Riviere, J. (1958) 'A character trait of Freud's', In J. Sutherland (ed.) *Psychoanalysis and Contemporary Thought*, London: Hogarth Press; also printed in J. Riviere *The Inner World and Joan Riviere – Collected Papers: 1920–1958*, London: Karnac, 1991.
Rorty, R. (1989) *Contingency, Irony, and Solidarity*. Cambridge: Cambridge University Press.
—— (1991) *Essays on Heidegger and others – Philosophical Papers*, Cambridge: Cambridge University Press.
Rosenfeld, H. (1947) 'Analysis of a schizophrenic state with depersonalisation', *International Journal of Psycho-Analysis* 17: 304–320; also reprinted in *Psychotic States – A Psychoanalytical Approach*, London: Hogarth Press, 1965.
—— (1952) 'Notes on the psycho-analysis of the superego conflict in an acute schizophrenic patient', in *Psychotic States – A Psychoanalytical Approach*, London: Hogarth Press, 1965 (reprinted 1982, London: Karnac).

—— (1983) 'Primitive object relations and mechanisms', *International Journal of Psycho-analysis* 64: 261–267.

—— (1987) *Impasse and Interpretation – Therapeutic and Anti-therapeutic Factors in the Psychoanalytic Treatment of Psychotic, Borderline, and Neurotic Patients,* London: Tavistock Publications.

Scarfone, D. (2002) 'It was *not* my mother: From seduction to negation', in *New Formations*, 48, 2002–2003.

Segal, H. (1950) 'Some aspects of the analysis of a schizophrenic', in *The Work of Hanna Segal – A Kleinian Approach to Clinical Practice*, New York: Jason Aronson, 1981.

—— (1957) 'Notes on symbol formation', in *The Work of Hanna Segal – A Kleinian Approach to Clinical Practice*, New York: Jason Aronson, 1981.

Tausk, V. (1919) 'On the origin of the "influencing machine" in schizophrenia', in R. Fliess (ed.) *The Psycho-Analytic Reader – An Anthology of Essential Papers with Critical Introductions*, London: Hogarth Press, 1950.

Thompson, M. G. (1994) *The Truth about Freud's Technique – The Encounter with the Real*, New York and London: New York University Press.

Winnicott, D. W. (1945) 'Primitive early development', in *Collected Papers: Through Paediatrics to Psycho-Analysis,* London: Tavistock Publications, 1958 (reprinted 1992, London: Karnac).

—— (1947) 'Hate in the counter-transference', in *Collected Papers: Through Paediatrics to Psycho-Analysis*, London: Tavistock Publications, 1958 (reprinted 1992, London: Karnac).

—— (1949 [1954]) 'Birth memories, birth trauma, and anxiety', in *Collected Papers: Through Paediatrics to Psycho-Analysis,* London: Tavistock Publications, 1958 (reprinted 1992, London: Karnac).

—— (1954) 'Metapsychological and clinical aspects of regression within the psycho-analytical set-up', in *Collected Papers: Through Paediatrics to Psycho-Analysis*, London: Tavistock Publications, 1958 (reprinted 1992, London: Karnac).

—— (1960) 'Counter-transference', in *The Maturational Processes and the Facilitating Environment: Studies in the Theory of Emotional Development*, London: Hogarth Institute of Psycho-Analysis, 1965 (reprinted 1990, London: Karnac).

—— (1962) 'Ego integration in child development', in *The Maturational Processes and the Facilitating Environment: Studies in the Theory of Emotional Development*, London: Hogarth Institute of Psycho-Analysis, 1965 (reprinted 1990, London: Karnac).

—— (1963 [1974]) 'Fear of breakdown', in C. Winnicott, R. Shepherd and M. Davis (eds) *Psycho-Analytic Explorations*, London: Karnac, 1989.

—— (1965) 'The psychology of madness – a contribution from psycho-analysis', in C. Winnicott, R. Shepherd, and M. Davis, (eds) *Psycho-Analytic Explorations*, London: Karnac, 1989.

C. Winnicott, R. Shepherd, and M. Davis, (eds) (1989) *Psycho-Analytic Explorations*, London: Karnac. z

Index

acting out 49, 77, 95
aggression 18, 21, 25
Alford, C. F. 95
alpha elements 21
ambivalence 11
analytic impasse 93
analytic relationship 7, 8, 19–20, 79, 80, 81–2
anti-psychiatry movement 87, 88
at-one-ness ix, xv
attachment 6, 13
Aulagnier, Piera 63, 70, 77

Balint, E. 91
Balint, M. 6, 20
Barfield, Owen xiii, xvi
'benevolent neutrality' 20, 96n5
Bergmann, Martin 6, 21
betrayal 12, 14
Bion, Wilfred xi, 6, 21, 48, 87, 90, 91
bisexuality 17, 30, 32, 37
Blanchot, Maurice xii
Bleger, José 87, 93, 97n6
body 14, 54
borderline pathology 73, 90
bouffées delirantes 89
Bowlby, J. 6, 21
Brahma 27–8
breast 12, 25, 63, 64, 65
Breuer, J. 4

Britton, R. 96n5
Burrow, Colin xi, xiv
Byatt, A. S. 66

castration 17, 47
cathexis 12–13, 16, 18
chastity 32, 34, 35
Cohen, T. 82–3
Coltart, Nina 85
communication 13, 14, 66
complicité 77, 82
conflict of suffering 84
coprophagy 75–6
the couch 91
countertransference 7, 19–20, 79, 80–1
courtly love 19, 32
cultural experience 9, 24
culture 10

David, Christian 27
death ix, x, 76; *The Phoenix and the Turtle* xiv, 31, 33–4, 37; psychosis 74
death drive 6
death instinct 12, 24, 94
defences 69
delusions: *bouffées delirantes* 89; experience of love 16; psychosis 69, 71; Tony's case xiv, xv, 52, 53, 61, 62

depression 61, 83–4
desire x, xi–xii, 17; for the breast 65; Lacan 25; persecutory 46; sexual ix, xi, 3
destruction ix, x, xiv–xv; Eros 6; French psychoanalysis 25; Klein 6; sexuality relationship 21; Winnicott 24
destructiveness 21, 23, 77, 80, 90, 95
desubjectivation 94
detachment 81, 82
dreams xvi, 48, 52, 56, 78, 86
drives 6, 12, 13, 23, 24–5, 69; *see also* instincts
drug use 44, 87, 89

ego 4, 12–13, 14, 25
egotism xii
envy 78, 80
Eris 12
Eros x, xii; Freud 3, 4, 6, 9, 13, 16; madness xvi, 69
eroticism 19
Everett, Barbara xiii

Fairbairn, W. R. D. 21
fantasies 24, 52, 68, 74, 76, 78
fear 43, 67, 94
Ferenczi, S. 8, 21
frame 93
French psychoanalysis 25–7
Freud, Sigmund 3–4, 9, 15–16, 64, 83; aggression 21; 'benevolent neutrality' 96n5; breast 12; 'choice of neurosis' 95; conflict of suffering 84; drives 12, 13; French psychoanalysis 25–7; hatred of reality 90; helplessness 62; love/hate fusion 23–4; non-unity of self 85–6; Oedipal structure 17; patient's motivation for treatment 85; primary processes 37; Rat Man case 24, 95; reliable character 85; Riviere 84; sexuality 5–6, 19, 20, 23, 25–6, 27; transference love 7–8, 19, 72–3, 81
friendship 9
fusional love 35–6

Gabel, J. 75
gender xi, 37
Greek mythology x–xi, 12
Green, André ix–xv, xvi, xvii, 1–39, 68, 69
grief xii
guilt 60, 76

hainamoration x, 6, 16, 25, 26
hallucinations 63, 69, 89; 'moments of illusion' 92; Tony's case 44, 46, 49, 52, 62
hate x, xiv–xv, 6, 17; countertransference 7, 20, 81; *hainamoration* x, 6, 16, 25; infant fantasies 68; *jouissance* 26; love relationship 21, 23–4; psychotic love-hate confusion 74; symbolically impoverished patients 47; transference 8; transformation of love into 12
Heimann, Paula 7
helplessness 13, 62, 63, 68
homosexuality 46
hostility 17, 18, 24
humility 84, 85
humour 57, 82–3
hunger 12
hyperconsciousness 55
hysteria 89–90

idealisation 5, 11, 32, 49, 71; admiration for love object

23; of analyst 78, 79; illusion distinction 16, 24; 'normal madness' 69
identification 17, 68
illusion 16, 24, 92, 93
immortality 30, 31, 32
incest 45, 46
infant–mother relationship xvi, 17–18, 23, 27, 36, 62–71; *see also* mother
infantile experience xvi, 10, 15
infantile love 9, 20, 23, 27
infantile sexuality 17, 20, 26, 27
instincts 3, 4, 24; *see also* drives
inter-subjective school 81
introjection 8, 79
intromission 70
introspection 55
irony 57, 84

jealousy 12, 14, 58–9
jouissance x, 26, 31

Keats, John ix, xv, 32
Kernberg, O. 6
Klein, Melanie 17, 24, 87; the breast 64; destruction 6, 21; Oedipus complex 67; psychoanalytic technique 91
Knight, G. Wilson 31–2, 33, 36
Kohon, Gregorio x, xi, xii, xvi–xviii, 41–100
Kristeva, J. 77–8

Lacan, Jacques 21, 25–6, 82; *hainamoration* x, 6, 16, 25; *jouissance* x, 26; language 65; mirror stage 67; Oedipus complex 67
Laing, R. D. 76, 88
language 25, 65, 66, 73
Laplanche, Jean 27, 62, 63, 65, 70, 95
Laufer, E. 23
Laufer, M. 23

laughter 57, 82–3
learning x, 64–5, 94
Leidenskonflikt 84
length of sessions 91–2
libido 3, 78, 81
literature x, xiii, 5, 10, 83
Loewald, H. 77
loneliness xii
love at first sight 11, 15

MacAlpine, Ida 18
McDougall, Joyce 27
madness ix–x, xii, 23, 95, 96; definition of 69–70; fear of xvii–xviii, 96; normal xvi–xvii, 68–70, 71, 72; 'original' 68–9; Tony's case xvi–xvii, 46, 56, 58; *see also* psychosis; schizophrenia
masochism 24, 78
masturbation 52, 76
'maternal madness' 27
Meltzer, Donald 8, 21
memories 43, 86
A Midsummer Night's Dream 14–15
mirror stage 67–8
'moments of illusion' 92, 93
Money-Kyrle, R. 96n5
moral character 85
mother: infant relationship xvi, 17–18, 23, 27, 36, 62–71; intromission 70; 'moments of illusion' 92; Mr R's case 75; *Mutter Komplex* 18; omnipotence of 63, 68; pathologically disturbed 70–1; phobia of 74; sexuality xvi, 23, 27; Tony's case 43–5, 53–4, 56–61, 71–2, 83, 86–7, 96; *see also* Oedipus complex
mourning 17, 24, 36–7
murderous feelings 46, 49–50, 55, 57, 59

music 83
Mutter Komplex 18
mysticism 5, 32
mythology x–xi, 12, 30, 33

narcissism 9, 12, 16; of analyst 79; hatred differentiation 17; Lacan 25; mirror stage 67–8; 'normal madness' 69; *The Phoenix and the Turtle* 37; primary 3, 6, 20, 24
negativity 55, 77, 82
neo-Kleinians 17, 24
neurosis 91, 95
Nietzsche, F. W. 29, 32
nostalgia 14, 23

objects 3, 11–12, 13, 14, 16; admiration for love object 23; Bion 90; cathexis 12–13, 16, 18; Klein 68; murderous attacks by 80; new discovery of 77; object choice 6, 95; persecuting 52, 54, 67; transference love 9
Oedipus complex 17–18, 24, 67, 71–2; *see also* mother
omnipotence 55, 63, 68, 76, 84
'original madness' 68–9
Ovid xi

panic 74
paranoid schizophrenia 44, 61–2
passion ix–x, xiv, xv, 10, 34, 35–6
Peirce, C. S. 18
perception 54–5
The Phoenix and the Turtle x, xi, xiii–xiv, xv, 28–37
Pichon-Rivière, Enrique 41, 87–8, 93
Plato 11, 32
platonic love 19, 32
poetry xi, xii, xiii–xiv, 5, 28–37
Pontalis, J.-B. 62, 63, 95
possession xvii, 14, 16

power 78
primary communication 14
primary processes xiii, 14, 36, 37, 62
Prince, F. T. 32–3
projection 79
projective identification 16, 48–9, 79, 88
psychiatry 87, 88
psychic space 81
psychoanalytic setting 92, 93
psychological mindedness 86
psychosis: analytic interpretation 60; *bouffées delirantes* 89; countertransference 80–1; hysterical 89–90; insights into own madness 88–9; Laing 88; love-hate confusion 74; madness distinction 69; mother–baby relationship 70–1; psychiatric patients 87; psychic agony 73; recovery 77, 92; Tony's case 47, 48, 52–3, 60, 62, 93–4; *see also* schizophrenia
puberty 20, 23

Racine, Jean x–xi, 1, 10
Rank, O. 8
regression 58–9
'reliable character' 85
religion 5, 22
Renik, Owen 20
reparation 24
repetition 19, 23, 77
repression 10, 12
revelation 11
Riviere, Joan 21, 24, 84
Rosenfeld, Herbert 21, 74, 78–9, 80, 87, 91, 93

sadism 21, 90
schizophrenia 74–6; diagnosis of 89; psychoanalytic

techniques 91; Tony's case 44, 47, 50, 55, 61; transferences 87–8; *see also* psychosis
science xiii, 5, 22
Segal, Hanna 47, 87, 91
self: Freud 85–6; institutionalised 94; self-other boundaries 47
self-love 9
self-sacrifice xi, 12, 17
sensuality 6, 9, 20, 23
separation 12, 13, 14, 16, 90
sexual desire ix, xi, 3
sexual drives 4, 13, 16
sexual fulfilment xii
sexuality 19, 20–1, 22–3; French psychoanalysis 25–7; Freud 3, 5–6, 25–6; hostility 24; intromission 70; 'normal madness' 69
Shakespeare, William x–xii, xiii–xiv, xvi, 1, 10, 28–37
shame 79–80
sibling rivalry 57
significant others 65, 67
signs 65
Spenser, Edmund 32
splitting 48, 77
Stoller, Robert 24
'subjective disparity' 82
subjectivity 65, 66, 67, 68, 69, 94
sublimation 5, 16, 23, 32
suffering 84
suicide 76
Surgeon, Caroline 29
symbolisation 11, 68
symbols xvi, 47

tenderness 6, 9, 17, 20, 23

terror xiv, xv, 74, 76
'third term' 18, 53, 68, 92–3
Thompson, Guy 85
transference 7–9, 18–19, 20, 73, 81; idealisation 78, 79, 90; 'normal madness' 72; object relations 90; psychotic patients 77–8; repetition 19, 23, 77; schizophrenic patients 87–8; Tony's case 46, 47; *see also* countertransference
transference love xiv, 7–10, 18–19, 60; Freud 7–8, 19, 72–3, 81; helplessness 13; 'normal madness' 69, 72
transitional space 51, 68
trauma 62, 70, 73, 93
triangulation relationship 18
the unconscious 25, 36, 65, 73, 81

Vaterkomplex 17
Venus and Adonis xi, xii, 1
violence 23, 63
vulnerability 78, 80, 90

Waddell, Margot ix–xviii
Weiss, Edoardo 84
Widlöcher, D. 20
Williams, Meg Harris xi
Winnicott, D. xvii, 21, 64, 77; countertransference 20; distance between analyst and patient 82; drives 24–5; illusion 16, 24, 92; madness xvii, 69, 96; psychoanalytic technique 91; refutation of death drive 6

For Product Safety Concerns and Information please contact our EU
representative GPSR@taylorandfrancis.com
Taylor & Francis Verlag GmbH, Kaufingerstraße 24, 80331 München, Germany

www.ingramcontent.com/pod-product-compliance
Lightning Source LLC
Chambersburg PA
CBHW070629300426
44113CB00010B/1713